Learning and Teaching in Adult Education

CW01091419

Study Guides in Adult Education

edited by
Regina Egetenmeyer

Henning Pätzold

Learning and Teaching in Adult Education
Contemporary Theories

Barbara Budrich Publishers
Opladen & Farmington Hills, MI 2011

A CIP catalogue record for this book is available from
Die Deutsche Bibliothek (The German Library)

© 2011 by Barbara Budrich Publishers, Opladen & Farmington Hills, MI
www.barbara-budrich.net

ISBN   978-3-86649-443-5

Die Deutsche Bibliothek – CIP-Einheitsaufnahme
Ein Titeldatensatz für die Publikation ist bei Der Deutschen Bibliothek erhältlich.

Verlag Barbara Budrich Ⓑ Barbara Budrich Publishers
Stauffenbergstr. 7. D-51379 Leverkusen Opladen, Germany

28347 Ridgebrook. Farmington Hills, MI 48334. USA
www.barbara-budrich.net

Institutional Editor: University of Duisburg-Essen, Germany
Jacket illustration by disegno, Wuppertal, Germany – www.disenjo.de
Copy-editing: Carsten Bösel
Typeset by Susanne Albrecht, Germany – www.lektorat-albrecht.de
Printed in Europe on acid-free paper by
paper&tinta, Warsaw

Contents

Part Two: The 'Art of Teaching': Exploring Concepts of Adult Learning to Address Didactic Challenges

Preface

In the last couple of months, I did several interviews with German adult education students who are currently studying abroad in Europe and the United States. Asked about their experiences in their host countries, many of them told me they were having a hard time explaining what adult education is all about, frequently encountering questions such as, 'Why should adults be learning? Adults have finished their schooling and vocational training – aren't they done with learning?' Some even told me they actually met people who saw no need whatsoever for offering adult education programmes.

Now this sounds very strange to the ears of German adult education students. Germany, after all, has had publicly funded adult education courses for about 90 years; for more than 40 years, there have been academic programmes designed to train adult education professionals. Adults do learn on a daily basis. But adult ways of learning are mostly discussed in other terms. Informal learning, for example, is called 'gaining experience', 'observing', 'reading', 'discussing', 'researching', or 'going by trial and error'. Organised learning arrangements are called 'human resource development', '(professionnal) training', 'coaching', 'mentoring', or 'attending conferences'.

To support these adult learning activities – which we call adult education – research shows that we need to adopt different approaches from those we employ to support the learning of children. Adults' conscious or unconscious decision for or against learning is crucially important here. Adults, after all, are not blank slates to simply be written on. They have developed structures and interpretation patterns with which they see the world. Relevance and personal meaning are more important. Adult educators, therefore, have to address the internal structures and interpretation patterns of their target group. They have to identify the aspects and topics that adult learners care about. They need to create connections between the learning subject and the knowledge, skills, and attitudes of the adult target group. In the context of adult education, these aspects are called 'target group orientation' and 'connectivity'.

In this study guide, Henning Pätzold provides an overview of key learning theories and what they mean in terms of teaching. In Part One, he presents a selection of learning theories drawn from the broad academic field of education, introducing readers to a variety of approaches for designing theories of adult learning: learning triangles, relational perspectives, logical models and stages, as well as comprehensive approaches. The presentation includes learning theories developed by scholars from several countries, thereby providing an insight into different international learning theories. Henning Pätzold takes these theories to serve as basis for Part Two of his book, which is focused on didactics, or adult teaching methods. Here, he illustrates some of the practical implications of the learning theories presented in Part One. According to the author, the following aspects are central for adult learning arrangements: reflection, time, person, and lifeworld.

Henning Pätzold has been studying international learning theories for several years and has taught the subject multiple times as an online module within the European Master in Adult Education programme in Duisburg-Essen. As a result, some aspects presented in this study guide have already been tried out in practice. In the overall context of the Study Guides in Adult Education series, this guide has been designed to supplement and expand upon the ideas presented in the preceding volume by Paul Bélanger. My sincere thanks go to Henning Pätzold for his contribution to this series.

Regina Egetenmeyer

1. Introduction

'Nothing is as practical as a good theory.' The great theorist of psychology, Kurt Lewin, is said to have coined this statement, although it was probably made earlier. A sweeping proposition like this one certainly eases the work of the scholarly writer tremendously, since no justification or excuse has to be provided for filling shelf after shelf with sophisticated theoretical treatises, which all have to be regarded as 'practical' by their mere existence. There is more to Lewin's proposition, however, than merely rubber-stamping any theoretical effort whatsoever. Theory necessarily comes into play whenever routines and simple recipes turn out to be insufficient. Unfortunately, this situation is the rule rather than the exception in the field of adult education. After all, each teaching and learning situation is, first and foremost, an encounter with diversity. Participants meet each other, get to know the course contents, and meet the adult educator, who in turn encounters the participants and will probably also gain new perspectives on what he or she is teaching. These ingredients make up a complex social field which positively cannot be addressed by applying simple recipes.

In fact, such complexity lies at the core of the social sciences, which are sometimes rather derogatorily referred to as 'soft sciences'. However, as the well-known representative of constructivist thinking, Heinz von Foerster, who earned his first merits in the 'hard science' field of computer science, once put it, 'the hard sciences ... deal with the soft problems, the soft sciences ... deal with the hard problems' (von Foerster, 1972, p. 1). From a cyberneticist's point of view, a problem is hard if there are multiple solutions that cannot be precisely determined based on the given circumstances. Multiplying 100-digit numbers, for example, is a soft problem because there is only one solution; moreover, from a logical point of view, the corresponding equation is tautological. Developing a strategy to ease language learning for immigrants, in contrast, is a hard problem because (a) there are infinite numbers of possible solutions, and (b) we cannot determine which of them would work best based on the problem alone, not to mention the secondary effects each of them might have on other areas of social life. Science deals with such complexity through theory. And theory is designed to reduce complexity to a degree that, on the one hand, covers the important aspects of an area of research, and, on the other hand, renders it manageable for further investigation, experiment and, eventually, application. This leads to an important qualifier in Lewin's statement: *good* theory is what is required.

> **Keyword: Learning theory**
>
> A theory (Greek: θεωρία) can be understood as a particular mode of looking at and describing a phenomenon. A scientific theory should consist of statements that are intersubjectively comprehensible and unambiguous. A learning theory thus should provide statements on learning which contribute to a comprehensive picture of learning, helping us to observe and describe the phenomenon of learning. By providing particular 'interpretations and understanding of educational practice' (Biesta, 2009, p. 2), such a theory may very well *support* such practice; however, it cannot serve as full *legitimisation* for any particular action.

A good theory of learning for adult education should reduce the complex phenomenon of (human) learning in a way that allows an adult educator to think about concrete ways to facilitate learning in classroom situations. There are numerous theories of learning, some of which are well known (e.g. behaviourism or cognitivism); however, as psychological theories, they serve a different purpose. Important as they are as theoretical points of reference, their usefulness is quite limited for planning or conducting courses, which is why this text touches on them only briefly (in Chapter 6) and does not try to present them from an adult education perspective. Readers interested in general learning theories are encouraged to consult other resources for more detailed explanations (e.g. Bélanger, 2011; LeFrançois, 2005). Instead, the first part of this book provides an insight into some of the major contributions to *learning theory with respect to pedagogy*. These contributions represent a variety of approaches which have been selected to not only cover the main currents of recent pedagogical learning theory, but also to be instructive with respect to managing learning from an adult educator's point of view. As a consequence, they address the phenomenon of learning from quite different angles, ranging from the emotional perspective and formal logic to comprehensive approaches. All in all, this part is intended to give an insight into how human learning is understood and discussed within adult education. However, any selection of major theoretical contributions may always be criticised for overlooking this or that approach or even a whole school of thinking. In this respect, the present study guide is no exception. Without a doubt, one may claim that certain positions not included here also deserve mentioning. Space, however, is limited. As a result, the selection presented here does not claim to be complete. Instead it has been designed to provide a coherent picture. There are other legitimate and important concepts that have not been included because they were not considered to contribute significantly to *this particular* picture – which is not at all to say their general quality is called into question.

Due to the nature of this study guide, the theories presented in Part One have been simplified to a considerable degree. While the more recent of them sometimes are merely based on a few articles or a single book, others have long since initiated a broad debate that has resulted in a wide range of projects, articles, and books. As far as possible, the following sections seek to capture the core ideas of each theory by referring to the basic texts and by providing some of the well-known figures for illustration. As a result, the theories become available for immediate pedagogical reflection. Furthermore, as in the other volumes of the study guide series, readers are supported in their reflections by a number of tasks and exercises at the end of each chapter.

Applying theoretical considerations is also the main focus of Part Two, which begins with an introduction to the usage of a somewhat difficult term: *didactic*. Although the term represents a rich and fruitful discussion throughout centuries of European thinking about education, didactics also has a negative connotation. Chapter 7 clarifies the term with respect to the context of this study guide. Furthermore, it provides an overview of some of the major didactic approaches, which may claim to represent different 'models' of teaching. The text will not give a comprehensive presentation of the main currents in didactic thinking with respect to such models, however. There are just too many of them – and, what is more important, even though they make constructive contributions to the discussion, these models and approaches usually cannot be regarded as *theories*. Therefore, they rather serve as further background for interpretation. The following chapter then goes on to discuss didactic implications from three perspectives, namely time, person, and life-world as the crucial characteristic conditions of human learning. Embracing these perspectives is intended to encourage and support didactic thinking that is related to practice and well grounded in theory. Therefore, instead of providing schemata or 'rules' for teaching, we shall look at time, person, and life-world to arrive at more general didactic conclusions, which I hope are still concrete enough to be useful for teaching. Moreover, they are intended to foster the mutual consideration of theory *and* practice.

Ralph St. Clair once reflected on this relationship, stating that theory and practice are prepared to maintain 'a beautiful friendship' (St. Clair, 2004). Following this metaphor, we might say that theory, on the one hand, shall not impose regulations on practice (and vice versa), but, as a good friend, insist on problematic issues even if this should initially irritate and complicate practice. Practical experience, on the other hand, shall always be prepared to challenge theory in case the latter just does not seem to pay attention anymore. St. Clair's study has not only provided us with a nice metaphor, it has also revealed an unexpected and encouraging fact: not only do practitioners use scientific contributions to their field, their usage even increases throughout the time they are working in the field – as long as they are equipped to fulfil the general preconditions: knowledge about ongoing research and proficiency in the corresponding professional terminology. This study guide, as the other volumes in this series, is designed to support readers in further developing both.

Part One:
Theories of Learning:
A Field of Approaches towards
the Learning of Adults

2. Of Learning Triangles and Beyond

2.1 Introducing systematic approaches

Triangles are often used to represent relationships in a plain and easy way, and education is no exception in this respect. In fact, one of the most common figures in education is the so-called *didactic triangle* (see Figure 1). It represents a quite general relationship between the learner, the teacher, and the issue. The model, of course, has undergone several alterations; recent concepts in particular emphasise the fact that the various relationships within the model are not of the same type. For example, according to a more andragogical concept, the teacher is a mere moderator of the relationship between the other two instances. We will refer to that later when discussing relational didactics (see Chapter 3).

Figure 1: Didactic triangle

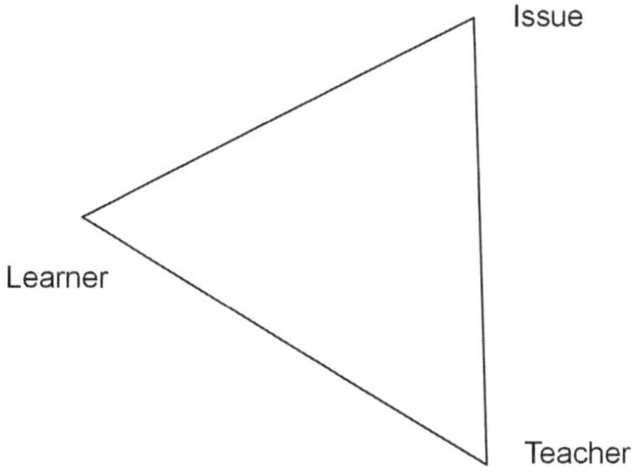

Source: Arnold & Pätzold, 2007, p. 95

Although the didactic triangle focuses on the three main structural entities in the learning-teaching-process, the learning triangle we will discuss in the following section is related to the learner (see Figure 2). Conceptualised by the

Danish educational scientist Knud Illeris, the learning triangle, too, has undergone several changes, but the core concept has remained the same. Basically, Illeris (2003, 2004, 2006) addresses three issues related to the learning of an individual:

- Learning takes place in a socio-cultural context.
- Learning has a cognitive dimension.
- Learning has an emotional (or psychodynamic) dimension.

> **Keyword: Socio-cultural context**
>
> Any learning activity is influenced by the fact that the learner is situated in some kind of context. This context consists of other persons as well as of a variety of cultural influences such as convictions, habits, rules, and so forth. In brief, the socio-cultural context can be defined as the various social and cultural factors that influence a particular learning process. (Obviously, it is not an easy task to identify those influences. It is all the more important, therefore, not to abstract from the socio-cultural context when discussing learning.)

Although the first issue is frequently considered in theories of social learning, it tends to be underestimated in more psychologically oriented contributions to learning theory (see Schäffter, 2010, p. 297). The second and third issues resemble the concept of cognitive and affective learning goals, which were first addressed in the second half of the twentieth century. What is important to point out here is that Illeris rejects the idea of separating cognitive learning processes on the one hand from affective or emotional ones on the other. When it comes to learning, emotions and cognition rather are two sides of the same coin. They are always affected simultaneously, regardless of whether the subject matter is intended to affect one side more than the other. However, they serve different functions: Whereas the cognitive side leads to knowledge and skills, enabling the individual to 'function' (Illeris, 2004, p. 94), the emotional or psychodynamic side (Illeris uses both terms) serves to maintain a balance between inner and outer world and therefore to establish *sensitivity* (ibid.) – that is, the ability to react to external stimuli in nuanced and adequate ways with regard to emotions.

Figure 2: Illeris's learning triangle

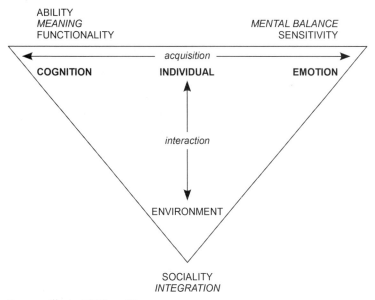

Source: Illeris, 2004, p. 95

The social dimension is characterised by our aim to integrate ourselves into certain social contexts. Although learning may be seen as an individual process of balancing emotional and cognitive aspects, it is always in some way related to the environment. Therefore, the process of learning consists of two simultaneous processes: a process of interaction, in which learning mediates between the individual and his or her social environment (cf. Geulen & Hurrelmann, 1980, p. 51), and a process of acquiring knowledge and skills as an evolution of cognitive and emotional perspectives towards the subject matter.

From the perspective of systems theory, we may now ask about the precise nature of the individual that Illeris places in opposition to its social environment. Niklas Luhmann describes this interaction as a process that can be observed in the social world, yet the relationship between interaction and individual is a matter of different kinds of observation and attribution (cf. Luhmann, 1995, p. 256). Moreover, the rather psychological terms of emotion and cognition raise the question of whether the body of the individual may already be regarded as some type of environmental condition (ibid, p. 262). Generally, this question draws our attention to the fact that the body is not a main focus in Illeris's concept. But we may, for the moment, translate *individual* freely with *person* and come back to that point later, especially as Illeris claims to cover the concept of *personal development* (Illeris, 2006, p. 30) within his approach. With that in mind, his theory already prepares us for dealing with the conceptual framework designed by Jarvis (see Chapter 5.1), who emphasises that it is 'the person who learns' (Jarvis, 2006, p. 32). The person learns within a social world, however, and Illeris introduces the notion of *sociality* to point out that this social world shall offer desirable prospects.

The process of *acquisition* is an interplay between the poles of cognition and emotion. Illeris uses these terms in a rather metaphorical way. The cognitive dimension means that the individual develops the ability to construct meaning (of things, facts, or situations) and therefore to function as a person. Note that 'functioning' in this context does not mean subordinating oneself to foreign purposes, but being able to think and act according to one's own goals. The emotional dimension relates to an individual's feelings, which accompany any learning process. Again, Illeris refers to the whole *psychodynamic dimension* (Illeris, 2006, p. 31) – that is, 'mental energy, feelings, and motivations' (ibid.).

From an analytical point of view, it may seem useful to separate the internal process of acquisition from the social process of interaction between individual and environment. Yet, for a comprehensive picture of learning, both of them have to be considered simultaneously. They serve as a kind of scaffolding for describing a learning process or a learning episode. For example, if we explore the role of motivation (which is part of the emotional pole in Illeris's model) within the theory of self-determination (Ryan & Deci, 2000), it seems that motivation depends considerably on the extent to which a particular environment offers opportunities to experience autonomy.

2.2 Levels of energy

Against this background, Illeris focuses on the process of acquisition and describes four distinct types or levels of learning with respect to the amount of change and psychic effort they require. His typology closely resembles the thinking of Gregory Bateson, who explored a similar general idea (see Chapter 4). Yet it also introduces the additional thought of relating different levels of learning to different biographical phases. Moreover, by explicitly referring to Mezirow's concept of transformative learning and Piaget's developmental approach, it is linked to two other important taxonomic approaches of learning.

Figure 3: Levels of learning

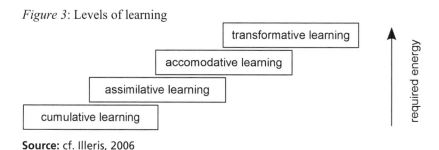

Source: cf. Illeris, 2006

The most simple type, 'cumulation or mechanical learning' (Illeris, 2004, p. 96) denotes the isolated acquisition of bits of information. Illeris states that although this type is dominant among children, it is less important for adults (except when memorising a phone number and the like). Yet research shows that cumulative learning is of high *systematic* importance even among adults: memorising plays a crucial role in learning foreign languages, for example. The next two types are denoted in terms borrowed from Jean Piaget: assimilative learning and accommodative learning. The former is described as the most common type of learning; it is also the usual way of learning at school. On this level, new information is integrated into existing concepts without challenging their core structure. Compared to cumulative learning, it can be imagined as not only piling up information, but also as sorting it according to a pre-existing system. Learning to use a new technical device, for example, often falls into this category. Although the specific procedures to operate the device may differ in detail, they are usually still similar to those used to operate previous versions of the device. The third type, accommodation, in contrast, requires more effort as it affects the system of knowledge itself. As described by Piaget, accommodation means not only to acquire new information, but also to reshape the existing system of concepts in a certain domain, as the new information will not comply with the old structure and, even when it does, cannot be neglected. Learning new theories, for example, often requires us to temporarily 'forget' what other theories say about the same issue, and to start rethinking the matter 'from scratch' instead. Illeris's fourth type of learning goes beyond Piaget's model and is linked to Mezirow's concept of transformative learning (ibid, p. 97). Mezirow himself distinguishes between two types of transformative learning: the 'transformation of patterns of meaning' (Mezirow, 1997, p. 78) questions the interpretational background against which new experiences or insights are processed. It therefore resembles Piaget's concept of accommodation. But to the extent to which transformation also affects the very person of the learner, it may go beyond accommodation. In this case, Mezirow speaks of 'perspective transformation' (ibid.), which is the deepest change an individual may undergo within the process of learning. Here, one's own 'perspectives of meaning' (ibid., p. 38) are fundamentally transformed: basic convictions and beliefs are profoundly changed against the background of new experiences. Therefore this type of learning is often associated with life crises.

Different taxonomies of learning, such as those of Mezirow and Illeris, are not identical, but they share a number of core ideas:

- Learning experiences can vary in depth.
- These variations are related to the extent to which the learning experience affects the whole person (identity, values, etc.).
- The depth of the learning process, therefore, is also related to its sustainability.

Accordingly, transformative learning requires more mental energy and deeply affects a learner's cognitive and emotional processes at the same time. Evidently, this often leads to changes in the learner's social environment as well.

What we can learn from Illeris's approach in terms of arriving at a comprehensive understanding of adult learning is that any type of learning may turn out to be relevant for the development of competence. The different levels build upon each other, even though they are not meant to form a particular hierarchy in which on type of learning is more valuable than another. Moreover, there is a considerable degree of overlap: transformative learning, for example, may contain aspects of all of the other levels of learning described above. We will return to this concept in Chapter 4.2.

Exercises and tasks

Exercise 1

In this chapter, the expression 'levels of energy' is used in a somewhat metaphorical way. What types of (physical or mental) energy might play a role with respect to the different levels of learning?

Exercise 2

What may *provide* the energy to sustain difficult learning processes? Think of personal examples.

Exercise 3

At the beginning of this chapter, it was said that memorising phone numbers could be regarded as cumulative learning. However, can you imagine conditions and situations in which it may be more than just that?

Task 1

Have a look at the self-determination theory of motivation by Ryan and Deci (see source below). How may the influences on motivation mentioned there have an impact on each of the four levels of learning depicted in Figure 3?
Ryan, R. M., & Deci, E. L. (2000). Self-determination theory and the facilitation of intrinsic motivation, social development, and well-being. *American Psychologist, 55(1)*, 68–78.

3. Relational Perspectives on Learning

When comparing Illeris's approach to the didactic triangle, we find that his emphasis is on the learner. Furthermore, by paying special attention to the general relationship between the learner and others, he mainly looks at the *social* aspects of learning. A different approach will investigate the relationship between the learner and the issue. From the variety of approaches to capture this relationship, we will now take a closer look at phenomenography (cf. Marton, 1992) and the concept of relational didactics (cf. Gieseke, 2007).

3.1 Phenomenography

The phenomenographic approach originated from experiments in learning research: Ference Marton and his colleagues at Gothenburg University (Sweden) started out with the assumption that 'the most important form of learning involves changing the way a person experiences, conceptualizes, or understands a phenomenon' (Marton, 1992, p. 253). The core terms of this assumption – *experience, concept,* and *understanding* – should therefore be the main focus when conducting learning research. However, Marton and his colleagues were well aware that 'observing students engaged in studying is really not a very rewarding research method. There is simply not much to observe' (Marton & Säljö, 2005, p. 40). Therefore they applied a qualitative research design in which students were asked to gain information out of text material presented to them. Afterwards, the results of this process were analysed with regard to learning outcomes and metacognitive dimensions (ibid., p. 41). This approach may seem rather conventional, but it marks an important shift away from other types of learning research. Instead of describing behaviour – by looking *at* individuals or *into* individuals, as it were, by analysing their mental or neuronal processes – Marton and his colleagues 'aim at an experiential description [...

and therefore] are trying to look *with* them and see the world as they see it' (Marton, 1992, p. 257). Furthermore, instead of looking at the efficacy of learning in terms of how much is learned (within a given time or effort), phenomenography 'seeks to investigate "what is learned" ' (Dahlgren, 2005, p. 27) in terms of a qualitative change in the person-world relationship.

Originally, the term *phenomenography* was used only to refer to the research method; later, it was also applied to the concept of learning implicit to this methodological design. As the concept places a strong focus on the *change* of concepts on the learner's side, the term *variation theory* is sometimes used as well.

The main results of their research led Marton and his colleagues to formulate a specific conception of learning that emphasises the three core terms mentioned above. Learning, in this perspective, consists of a change in

- the concepts learners have regarding a particular subject matter
- the understanding learners have of that matter
- the experiences learners have or may have with this matter.

Keywords: Concept, understanding, and experience in phenomenography

Concept in this context refers to an individual's idea of what belongs to an entity and what kind of relationship exists between its parts. Understood as a kind of inner representation of an external phenomenon, the term is used very much the way we use it in everyday speech. The term *understanding*, in contrast, has a more specific meaning within phenomenography or variation theory: it addresses the possible experiential relations between a person and a phenomenon. Understanding, in other words, shapes the ways in which we can relate ourselves to the outer world of experience (Marton, 1992). Consequently, *experience* means the factual realisation of the person's encounter of the phenomenon against the background of his or her concept and understanding.

An important idea in phenomenography is that understanding is a process between the individual and the *decontextualised* phenomenon; once understanding is gained, it refers only to the phenomenon and is not bound to a particular context or situation:

What we end up with is the conclusion that different understandings of phenomena are not specific to particular contexts, although they cannot occur other than in *some* context, and they are not specific to particular psychological acts, although they cannot occur other than in *some* psychological act. On the other hand, they *are* specific to the particular phenomenon of which they are understandings. (Marton, 1992, p. 261)

Hence, in this particular meaning, understanding is regarded as a 'nonpsychological category' (ibid, p. 262).

The third crucial term is *experience*. Here, the focus is on the actual encounter of the phenomenon and the learner. As stated above, this encounter is predetermined by understanding. Again, we refer to one of the original assumptions. Marton and Säljö argued that 'if the outcome of learning differs between individuals, then the very process of learning which leads to different outcomes must also have differed' (2005, p. 40). In other words, the students must have had different experiences. But although there is a virtually infinite number of possible experiences one can have with a phenomenon, Marton and Pang (1999) argue that this diversity of experiences can be reduced to clusters:

Every phenomenon can be experienced in a finite number of qualitatively different ways. In order to characterize the variation in ways people experience various phenomena, it is important to understand what it means to experience a phenomenon in a particular way. (p. 4)

Combining all of these considerations, the phenomenographic approach comes up with a specific idea of learning: learning is the change that occurs in a person's concepts, understandings, and experience with respect to a particular phenomenon. This change may be observed by distinguishing between a limited number of different understandings. (The number is limited when we only distinguish between qualitative differences.)

The phenomenographic theory of learning may be applied to a physical object, let's say a thermostat, for example. Although there is a variety of possible understandings of a thermostat as a valve, the basic idea is the same: a thermostat would be regarded as some passage of variable size allowing a certain amount of hot water to pass. A qualitatively different understanding of a thermostat would be that of a control circuit: based on a certain setting, a mechanism inside the thermostat automatically regulates the amount of water passing into the heating system by measuring the surrounding temperature. Again, there would be different ways of imagining this particular mechanism, but they all share the same basic idea.

The idea of a limited variety of qualitatively distinguishable understandings of a phenomenon also holds with respect to social or cultural phenomena. As another example, we might look at our understanding of morality. Since Piaget's and Kohlberg's efforts, empirical research has shown that people tend to argue about moral decisions against the background of a particular concept of morality, which usually changes over the course of one's personal development. From the early stages, in which morality is merely regarded as abiding by rules that were set by others, it evolves into concepts of a morally adjusted social community and, finally, into an individual set of well-founded values and norms.

The example regarding the evolution of moral judgement not only shows how the idea of qualitatively distinguishable concepts has proven fruitful in other branches of the social sciences, it also provides another example of how a learning process can be framed as a series of sequential steps along the lines of Illeris's four levels of learning. In this context, the phenomenographic approach can be applied to itself, resulting in a sequence of distinct *concepts of learning*, which may be compared to other hierarchies (see Chapter 4). The original results produced five such concepts of learning, but eventually Marton et al. added a sixth one (see Figure 4).

Figure 4: Levels of learning in the phenomenographic approach

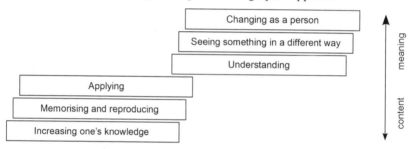

Source: cf. Marton, Dall'Alba, & Beaty, 1993, pp. 283ff.

Figure 4 shows that there is a kind of sequence from one level to another. Nevertheless, the model should not be confused with fixed sets of developmental stages (as in the example of developing moral judgement), because all levels may occur simultaneously or in a different sequence in certain learning processes, depending on which aspect of dealing with content is actually observed. There is a 'watershed' (Marton et al., 1993, p. 288), however, between the first three levels and the second three. Whereas the former three deal with the mere acquisition of content (including its more or less uncritical application), the latter three always relate to meaning.

The first level, *increasing one's knowledge*, simply means gathering new information that does not in any way interfere with one's existing knowledge. This may happen, for example, when we incidentally learn about the specific location of a room inside a building. *Memorising and reproducing*, in our example, would mean trying to memorise the position of certain rooms in a building, maybe by using a floor plan. The next level, *applying*, differs from the previous one in that knowledge is applied. (In our example, we might try to create our own floor plan based on our knowledge of the building.)

As stated above, meaning only plays a minor role in those processes. This changes as soon as we get to *understanding*, or, as Marton and Säljö have called it elsewhere, 'the abstraction of meaning' (2005, p. 55). As pointed out above, understanding is a core term in the theory of phenomenography, and once more the focus is on this particular type of learning, in which knowledge is processed in ways that are not completely foreseeable (as is more or less the case with the first three levels). Consequently, the remaining two levels go further into that direction: *seeing something in a different way* already affects the core of the person-phenomenon relationship, and *changing as a person* eventually expands the possible impact of learning to include any relevant process of human change.

Phenomenography, or variation theory, links some more or less analytically oriented approaches of learning theory and research (e.g. a system of levels of learning) with the philosophical tradition of phenomenology. At the same time, it tries to establish an alternative to psychological concepts of learning and is quite suitable for drawing didactic conclusions (see Part Two). This puts phenomenography in line with an arguably underestimated theoretical framework that aims to capture the human phenomenon of learning from a qualitative perspective without abandoning the methodological and analytical standards of contemporary social science (see also Göhlich & Zirfas, 2008; Jarvis, 2006, 2009; Meyer-Drawe, 2008; Roth 2004).

3.2 Relational didactics

Our starting point, the didactic triangle, suggested that pedagogical situations can *always* be seen from a relational perspective. As with other theories of networks, systems, and so forth, this is basically done by putting the focus on the edges of the model instead of putting it on the nodes. Viewed in this light, any didactic model can be regarded as relational (cf. Lund, 2003). Yet the term *relational* is used in a number of specific theoretical efforts, from which the work of German adult education researcher Wiltrud Gieseke (2007) has been selected for the following section. Gieseke explores the idea of *relational didactics* from an adult education point of view. Furthermore, she thoroughly addresses the issue of emotions, which links her work to that of Illeris and others.

> **Keyword: Relation**
>
> A relation describes what lies *between* two entities, such as a learner and a learning matter. The two entities may change while the relationship remains the same. (If Paul is taller than Peter, for example, the relationship won't change if Paul grows even taller.) However, a change in the relationship necessarily means a change in at least one of the participating entities (e.g. a physical change of position or a mental change of convictions). Thus relations often are good tools for observing processes in which we expect changes to occur without knowing exactly where they may occur.

Gieseke looks at different types of relations in educational situations. One is the relation between the learner and the learning matter; the other is the relation between the learner and any kind of society that forms a frame around learning situations. (The former resembles the approach of phenomenography, because significant learning is seen as a process in which people change their views towards something.) The concept of relational didactics links both types of relations:

Everything a human being calls learning throughout his life – usually indicating a different perspective on things, a further insight, a new skill, a change or extension in the long run – relies on relationships that have been established or can be established. (Gieseke, 2007, p. 216, own translation)

When we look at the relation between the individual and the learning matter, we find that Gieseke aims to go beyond the theoretical and methodological boundaries that often characterise psychological approaches towards learning, and the traditional philosophies of behaviourism and cognitivism in particular. She states that, from a psychological point of view, learning does not deal with different constellations of teaching and learning in general, but with different levels of learning (ibid., p. 222). These levels are covered more or less separately by different learning theories. Behaviourism, for example, mainly deals with learning processes related to the first two or three levels in the abovementioned hierarchy (see Figure 4). And although even behavioural psychology may legitimately claim that its theories do not end when it comes to meaning, the pedagogical perspective assumed here provides a different picture. Therefore Gieseke concludes that, from a pedagogical point of view, the struggle between different theories of learning is only a pseudo problem, as they only describe different types of learning.

Within this line of thought, learning by an individual eventually is considered to influence the whole person and, ultimately, society. Referring to the

German discussion, Gieseke contrasts her concept with that of *Bildung* (see also Chapter 7.1):

All participation in *Bildung* is an activity to change and to refine oneself. It has an impact on one's general condition and the whole potential of activities and judgements which take effect in a society. (Gieseke, 2007, p. 37, own translation)

Consequently, learning is rooted both in the individual and in the interaction between an individual and others. The latter aspect may cover the whole range of others, from a single individual to the learning group and society as a whole. Therefore, learning may be defined as 'a process of social exchange with more competent partners who enable us to reach new areas of development ...' (Rehrl & Gruber, 2007, p. 246, own translation). This idea is quite in line with classical philosophy: Aristotle, for example, saw society as the most powerful educator (cf. Göhlich & Zirfas, 2007, p. 66), and medieval philosophers put it in similar terms (ibid., p. 71). It is at this point that Gieseke's approach puts a specific focus on emotions. She emphasises that emotions are not only relevant for individual learning (fear, for example, tends to impede the acquisition of complex information), but even more so for modelling social interrelation in learning processes. 'Relations are ... emotionally situated' (Gieseke, 2007, p. 229); they provide 'the bridge to other people, which enables communication' (ibid., p. 15). Here, Gieseke argues against constructivism. In doing so, she is in good company: with the discovery of mirror neurons, recent research in neuroscience (the original provenance of constructivist theory) has enriched our understanding of the epistemological processes that occur in human interaction (cf. Gallese, 2005; Gallese, Keysers, & Rizzolatti, 2004; Pätzold, 2010a). Overall, Gieseke's thoughts provide a more comprehensive insight into the role of emotions in learning on the one hand, and the general idea of relations as a core analytical unit of learning processes on the other. Following this analytical perspective a bit further leads us to logical models that try to capture the phenomenon of learning in all of its complexity while still giving it a clear logical order.

Exercises and tasks

Exercise 1

Try to describe – in your own words – aspects of the relationship between phenomenography (variation theory) and phenomenology.

Exercise 2

Find examples from your own learning experience in which learning may be described as a change within a relationship.

Task 1

There are some good web resources to learn about phenomenography. At Phenomenology-Online, for example, you may start exploring some of the basic terms in the 'inquiry' section, which presents a variety of key terms such as 'embodied knowledge' or 'vocatio', as well as more general information on methods and procedures. After going through this material, you may want to revise your answers to Exercise 1.
http://www.phenomenologyonline.com

Task 2

The aforementioned article by Marton, Dall'Alba, and Beaty (see below) provides an insight into aspects of the research methodology of phenomenography. Read the article and discuss the opportunities and limitations of this research approach. Consider the complexity of learning and human development on the one hand, and the objective of generalising research results on the other.
Marton, F., Dall'Alba, G., & Beaty, E. (1993). Conceptions of learning. *International Journal of Educational Research, 19,* 277–300.

4. Logical Models and Stages of Learning

In previous chapters, we already came across a number of approaches that create hierarchies of learning (see Figure 4, for example). As there is obviously some kind of general principle underlying those concepts, we are going to investigate it further in this section. The core idea is to abstract from the particular learner and the particular content of learning to find a *logical* model of levels of learning. Learning theory and formal logic meet in two areas. On the one hand, there are several (mainly historical) contributions to logic which can also be read as contributions to learning theory (cf. Koch, 1988; Meyer-Drawe, 1996, 2003); on the other hand, concepts of formal logic can be utilised to describe learning in a particular way. They can result in models of logical types of learning, of which Gregory Bateson's (see below) might be the most prominent. Besides, other concepts of learning refer to formal logic (at least implicitly) when they arrange learning processes in a hierarchy, as we have seen with Illeris in Chapter 2. Similarly, concepts of human development, such as Piaget's, can be examined with respect to logical types. With Piaget, these concepts would include assimilation, accommodation, and the various stages of human development.

4.1 The relationship between logic and learning

With respect to the didactics of adult education, the German educational scientist Horst Siebert has called for a distinction between the *content-logic* (*Sachlogik*) of the learning matter, the *psycho-logic* (*Psychologik*) of the learner, and other factors (see Siebert, 2010, p. 14). Content-logic, which corresponds to the scientific system of a given discipline, is the result of a scientific discourse that involves more than just the respective experts.

Example: From a content-logic point of view, it is reasonable to classify plants by the number of their cotyledons (embryonic leaves) instead of, for example, the colour of their blossoms. Whereas the former is constant among all representatives of a genus (and beyond), the latter may vary even within a single species. Nevertheless, our psycho-logic is oriented at everyday experience, in which plants are usually identified by their blossoms, and the time to count the cotyledons has long passed. An instructor teaching a course on plants who aims to integrate learners' everyday experience is therefore well advised to give room to the characteristics of blossom colour before providing other characteristics which may lead to deeper knowledge and eventually help learners to differentiate a much higher number of plants.

Although content-logic seems to be superior from a scientific point of view, it often is not if we consider the learner's process of acquiring knowledge and competencies. Furthermore, respecting the perspective of psycho-logic helps to decrease the knowledge gap between the learner and the teacher (which is particularly desirable in most adult education settings). Yet it must not be overlooked that the final aim of a course may often be to amend (and sometimes replace) popular knowledge with scientific knowledge and to make it accessible for informing learners' decisions and judgements.

Eventually the different logics resemble the different perspectives on the phenomenon presented in the previous chapter. In both cases, we see a kind of transition from a simpler to a more complex view. Learning, in other words, refers to logic in addressing some kind of progress in which different stages of learning may still be distinguished.

4.2 Bateson's levels of learning

Gregory Bateson, a British anthropologist, social scientist, linguist, and cyberneticist, designed a widely acknowledged system of learning levels in which levels are described from a purely formal point of view. According to Bateson, there are five different levels:

Zero learning is characterized by *specificity of response*, which – right or wrong – is not subjected to correction.

Learning I is *change in specificity of response* by correction of errors of choice within a set of alternatives.

Learning II is *change in the process of Learning I*, e.g., a corrective change in the set of alternatives from which choice is made, or it is a change in how the sequence of experience is punctuated.

Learning III is *change in the process of Learning II,* e.g., a corrective change in the system of *sets* of alternatives from which choice is made... .

Learning IV would be *change in Learning III,* but probably does not occur in any adult living organism on this earth. Evolutionary process has, however, created organisms whose ontogeny brings them to Level III. (Bateson, 1972, p. 293)

Learning 0, in other words, refers to a process in which someone or something (this level can be applied to machines as well) responds to a given stimulus in a particular way without arguing about their response. This may occur, for example, after animals have learned a new response to a stimulus in a behaviouristic setting. The English word *learning*, unlike its equivalents in many other languages, conveys this particular meaning in sentences such as, 'I have learned from the siren that a police car is approaching' (ibid., p. 284). So Learning 0 is the repeated constant response to a particular stimulus (and, as the name *zero learning* suggests, we often would not call this process learning at all). However, the resulting response may turn out to be wrong in the sense that it does not match a certain stimulus. We may, for example, mistake a burglar alarm for a police car siren and, reacting according to Learning 0 (e.g. turning around to see the police car), find out that there is none. If we, in that case, adjust our reaction to that stimulus with respect to future situations, we have approached the level of Learning I. According to Bateson, behaviouristic conditioning is a very common case of Learning I. Instead of showing a certain reaction to a stimulus (or none at all), the subject learns to react in alternative ways. Eventually, Learning 0 has undergone change, and the subject shows a different (but again stable) reaction towards certain stimuli.

Following this line of analysis, Learning II can be seen as a change in Learning I – that is, at this stage, the learner becomes conscious of *how* his or her Learning I takes place, which offers him or her the opportunity to actively change these patterns. Learning II therefore not only addresses the stimulus, but also pays attention to the context in which it appears, relating more to manners, habits, and the like than to single stimuli. In our example, Learning II could mean for us not only to stop turning around whenever we hear a siren, but to start thinking about what may have led us to our erroneous expectation of a police car. We may investigate other similar sources of misunderstanding and eventually change our general concepts of warning sounds and how to deal with them. As Learning II means a change in Learning I, which is routinely understood as 'normal' learning, Learning II is regularly referred to as 'learning to learn' (Bateson, 1972, p. 292; Pätzold, 2010b). Bateson also introduced the term *deutero-learning* (cf. Bateson, 1972, p. 292; Visser, 2003), which means secondary learning.

Keyword: Deutero-learning

Bateson's term for second-order learning has been taken up in a variety of disciplines, particularly with respect to change management. The crucial idea is that learning processes themselves often require some kind of 'supervision' by the individual. In this respect, deutero-learning means to reflect (and change) individual learning processes according to organisational circumstances. However, in Bateson's approach, the term denotes *any* type of learning that modifies Learning I.

The last (regular) level in Bateson's model formally refers to a change of Learning II, literally a change in how learning to learn takes place. Obviously this is not a very common process. As Learning III challenges learners' most fundamental assumptions, it poses a serious threat to the stability of their everyday routines, their routinised social relations, and, eventually, their identity. Then again, there are situations in which it is desirable or even necessary to undergo such changes. Learning III, therefore, is usually expected to take place in extraordinary situations such as psychotherapy, religious conversion, and the like. It is difficult, if not impossible, to find a consistent verbal description of the process itself. This is one reason why it is useful to apply logics to learning. From a logical point of view, Learning III means that the 'rules' of Learning II, the learner's character, and his or her self-experience as a learner become the subject of deliberate change. 'Changing such habits involves a profound redefinition of a person's character or self, the aggregate of his or her past deutero-learning' (Visser, 2003, p. 276). Bateson himself stated that Learning III is rare and that he never observed any species other than humans going through this process. In fact, he added Learning III to his model only later; originally, it consisted only of Levels 0 to 2. From a logical point of view, however, there is no limitation to a certain stage. Learning IV can *logically* be defined as learning of Learning III and so on. Bateson briefly mentions that Learning IV might be regarded as an interplay of ontogenesis (i.e. the development of an individual organism from the earliest stages to maturity) and phylogenesis (i.e. the evolutionary development and diversification of a species or group of organisms). In conclusion, the difficulties of imagining such a thing as Learning IV can be illustrated by means of a mathematical analogy:

To get a feeling for Bateson's perspective on levels of learning, we may compare them to Euclidean geometry. (Bateson himself did so, but the idea presented here is a bit different.) Let's imagine Learning 0 as a single point (or a bit). It is either there or it isn't, and its dimension is zero. Learning I, then, equates a straight line. In geometry, and in a metaphorical sense as well, a line is an object of dimension one. As Learning I offers different but equivalent opportunities for zero learning, the dots on a line are different, but at the same time, they are all related to each other in the same fundamental relationship. Consequently, Learning II may be seen as a two-dimensional plane. In contrast to a straight line, a plane provides the possibility for different lines. A single dot (Learning 0 in our way of speaking) can be part of different straight lines as reference systems within the overall system of the plane. From here, it is not too difficult to imagine Learning III as the three-dimensional space in which different planes may emerge with or without intersections. Based on our everyday experience, however, we find it much easier to imagine planes and their spatial features because we can draw them. And for most people, it is a challenging task to try to imagine, let alone describe, a 'room' of more than three dimensions. So in a way, Bateson's model complies quite well with our spatial experience, which may at least be used as a metaphor for the different levels of learning.

Bateson's levels of learning provide a kind of blueprint for other conceptions of putting learning processes into a hierarchy of complexity. Some approaches have already been mentioned, others, such as the concept of transformative learning, will be the subject of later sections. We should always keep in mind, however, that (adult) learners may frequently experience different stages of learning simultaneously.

4.3 Alternatives to Bateson's levels of learning

Of course, there is a variety of possibilities to modify or replace Bateson's model with other proposals. His purely logic and constructive approach may be replaced with a more empirical one, for example (as Piaget has done with respect to the development of thought and the two 'levels' of accommodation and assimilation). The descriptions of Bateson's levels may be altered and refined according to everyday learning situations to expand their rather technical focus. Even if we choose to follow the purely logical approach, we may try to apply alternative *types of logic* to the matter of learning to get different perspectives on learning in terms of conceptualisation and research.

Although alternative types of logic are too complex to be explored in any depth here, we still touch upon them briefly to illustrate the point that unconventional thinking may lead to quite stimulating results. In the area of logical reasoning, for example, we may come across what is known as *non-classical logic.* This branch of logic explores how our view on logical problems (and eventually our whole rational thinking) changes when we – as a thought experiment – disregard the logical rule that the answer to certain questions can only be *yes* or *no*. The German philosopher and logician Günther Gotthard (1991) introduced a third alternative, the *rejection value* (p. 61), which can be understood as a type of answer that rejects the question. With the help of this third answer value, situations in which a question is not appropriate within the given context may be handled within the logical system. In a classroom situation, for example, in which the 'feasible' alternatives are (1) being able to learn or (2) not being able to learn, possible rejections might include (3.1) refusing to learn or (3.2) refusing to show what one has learned. Moreover, any interpretation of this situation will be inappropriate unless those rejections are taken into account – as Luhmann has shown with respect to the educational system, for example (cf. Luhmann, 2004, p. 45).

From among the various alternations and alternatives to Bateson's taxonomy, we will finally highlight the Structure of the Observed Learning Outcome (SOLO) taxonomy by Biggs and Collis (cf. Dahlgren, 2005).

Keyword: SOLO taxonomy

In a way reminiscent of the phenomenographic approach, the SOLO taxonomy lists learning outcomes in an empirically based hierarchy of five levels of understanding. The first level, called *pre-structural*, describes the rejection or merely formal acquisition of what is learned. Items are learned, if at all, as disconnected bits. The second level, *uni-structural*, involves a first generalisation of what is learned, but only with respect to a single aspect of the learning matter. The third level, *multi-structural*, involves generalisation with respect to several aspects. Whereas the first level resembles Learning 0 in Bateson's model, the following two rather match Learning I. (We have to keep in mind, however, that now the focus is on the learner again, not on the learning process itself, as with Bateson.) The fourth level in the SOLO taxonomy is called *relational* and is characterised by generalisations and inductive conclusions within a given or expected context. We may situate this level at the threshold from Learning I to Learning II in Bateson's model. The fifth level, *extended abstract*, eventually means deduction and induction within and beyond a given or expected context; in certain cases, it may be the equivalent of what Bateson characterised as Learning II. The SOLO taxonomy, as most other models of classroom-based learning, does not address Learning III, which tends to be attributed more to therapeutic contexts.

The logical approach shows that there can be productive exchange between formal logical concepts and empirical considerations of learning. The results of this exchange can be utilised in various ways. For learning theory, it is immensely important to reflect on the analytical framework in which learning is conceptualised. As Gieseke pointed out, mixing up the contributions from different stages of the learning process in an unreflecting manner may result in dramatic misunderstandings and pointless debate. From a practical point of view, it may also be useful to observe one's own learning processes with respect to different levels of learning. Difficulties and resistance to learning, for example, often do not occur at the same level as the learning issue itself. Literacy is a prominent example: research has shown that adults in certain living conditions may be able to learn how to read and write, but at the same time, they are often unable to apply these skills outside the classroom. Becoming literate seems to have such a dramatic impact on their overall situation that they are virtually unable to use their newly acquired competencies (cf. Pätzold, 2004, pp. 123–124). We shall return to the practical perspective in Part Two of this study guide.

Exercises and tasks

Exercise 1

Find further examples of the thresholds between the various learning levels according to Bateson.

Exercise 2

How would you describe the different learning levels from a relational perspective (cf. Chapter 4)?

Task 1

Above, we used a mathematical analogy to illustrate the idea of levels of learning. The underlying model was that of a change in dimension, which is quite easy to describe but difficult to imagine. For a more in-depth introduction on how we perceive dimensions (and a few hours of inspiring reading), I recommend Edwin A. Abbott's classic novella *Flatland: A Romance of Many Dimensions* (Abbott, n.d./1884).

Task 2

Like many other models, the SOLO taxonomy is primarily related to class-room-based learning. Nevertheless, it should also be applicable to adult learn-ing in formal, non-formal, and informal contexts. Review the taxonomy and identify the changes and amendments that may be necessary to apply it in any of those situations. Halloway (n.d.) gives a brief overview of the concept; Biggs and Collis's book is the primary source for the SOLO taxonomy.

Halloway, W. (n.d.). *Quality learning with reference to the SOLO model.* Available from http://www.une.edu.au/education/research/bhutan/publications/bhutan-solo-halloway.pdf

Biggs, J., & Collis, K. (1982). *Evaluating the quality of learning: The SOLO tax-onomy.* New York: Academy Press.

5. Comprehensive Approaches

5.1 Towards a comprehensive theory of learning?

The theories presented up to this point have mainly focussed on specific dimensions of learning (the interplay between cognition and emotion, the relational perspective, etc.), but there are other authors who have tried to capture the entire phenomenon of learning in one single theory. Such proposals necessarily give the impression of being quite eclectic. As in other areas of knowledge, a single unifying theory of learning is not in sight. Nevertheless, comprehensive concepts sometimes provide good examples of middle range theories (Robert Merton). One of the best known approaches in this field is that of the British adult education researcher Peter Jarvis, who himself refers to his ongoing efforts as steps 'towards a comprehensive theory of human learning' (Jarvis, 2006).

Figure 5: Kolb's learning cycle

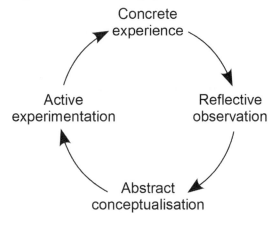

Source: Excerpt from Figure 2.4, Kolb, 1984, p. 33; see also Bélanger, 2011, p. 41

Jarvis's theory of learning originated in the 1980s, when he explored David Kolb's learning cycle (Figure 5) in a series of investigations. In these experiments, participants were given a printout of Kolb's model and asked to alter it according to their own learning experience. The idea was to eventually arrive at a more comprehensive and practical model. Although Jarvis's research would not satisfy modern methodological standards of qualitative research, it provided a good basis from which to further explore the processes of human learning from the actor's perspective. (Besides, as an easy and stimulating way to reflect on one's own learning experiences, Jarvis's proposal may still be used with great benefit in courses dealing with the learning of adults.)

Figure 6: The process of learning

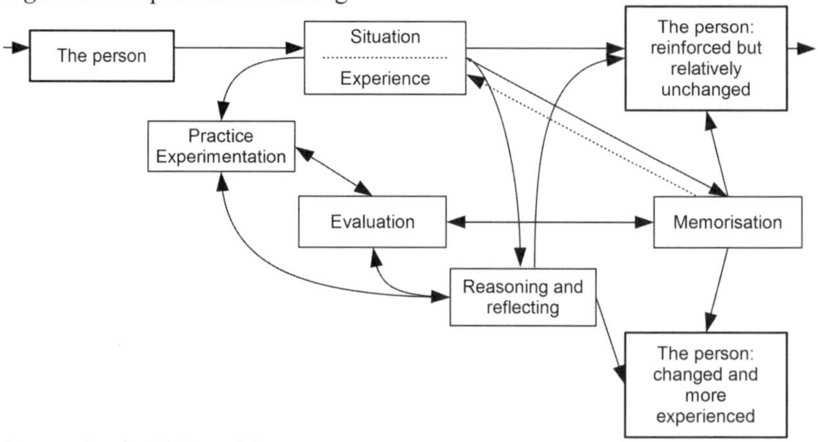

Source: Jarvis, 1987, p. 26

The results of Jarvis's investigations are shown in Figure 6. Although the two models seem to be quite different at first sight, there are meaningful similarities.

- In both models, learning is basically conceived as a circular process (see also Figure 7). This conception refers to the notion of a learning episode, which is quite common in psychology, for example. It may also be related to concepts such as Bateson's (see above), in which punctuation plays an important role in observing learning. Moreover, it is important when it comes to embedding 'small' learning processes in a broader context, such as lifelong learning.
- Both models feature the elements of experience, experimentation, and reflection.

- Although both models are more or less circular, experience plays a prominent role in both. In Kolb's model, it is put on top of the circle. Jarvis puts it in the same position and, although many elements may or may not be part of the learning process, the element 'situation/experience' is indispensable.

These similarities notwithstanding, there are obvious differences to be noted as well. First, Jarvis's model is a bit more complicated (and therefore lacks the elegance of Kolb's). This is due to the fact that, based on his respondents' statements, he broke down some of Kolb's steps into several parts. Furthermore, he added alternative paths between the various stages, allowing learners to bypass some of them or to go in circles within the model. Another important enhancement is the possibility for learners to go through part of the learning process *without* undergoing any particular change. In this case, Jarvis accordingly speaks of 'non-learning' (Jarvis, 2006, p. 10) – a possibility that is also considered in the work of Illeris (2003, p. 403) and further discussed in Chapter 8 of this study guide. Of Jarvis's various amendments to Kolb's model, that of memorisation deserves particular mention. From a theoretical perspective, it is possible to represent the process of memorisation as a specific form of learning within Kolb's model. Yet neither is it very elegant to do so, nor does it do justice to the eminent role of memorisation in many everyday learning processes, both formal and informal.

> **Keyword: Person**
>
> The Latin origin of the term refers to the mask of an actor. In modern theory, however, a person is defined as the irresolvable unity of body and mind.

In addition to refining Kolb's model, Jarvis stresses one essential point about learning: it is always the person who learns. Consequently, the learner must be placed at the beginning and at the end of any model of learning. By that, Jarvis underscores the idea that learning has to be conceptualised with respect to the learner as a person in the world rather than to any mental apparatus, cognitive system, brain, or other entity. This outlook goes back to Jarvis's early work on learning theory, but it has become even more important since. Thus Jarvis defines learning as

the combination of processes whereby the whole person – body (genetic, physical and biological) and mind (knowledge, skills, attitudes, values, emotions, beliefs and senses): experiences a social situation, the perceived content of which is then transformed cognitively, emotively or practically (or through a combination) and integrated into the person's individual biography resulting in a changed (or more experienced) person. (Jarvis, 2006, p. 13)

By placing the person at the centre, Jarvis is able to interpret other aspects of learning in more abstract ways than most psychological concepts. At the same time, this approach is testimony to his background as a sociologist: he describes learning as a change of the person or the self (Finger & Asún, 2001, p. 51), following the tradition of George Herbert Mead's symbolic interactionism. Figure 7 shows Jarvis's view of a person's transformation through learning. In its emphasis on the temporal change of the person rather than on the details of learning (or non-learning), it is obviously quite different from Kolb's learning cycle.

Figure 7: A learning episode as the transformation of a person

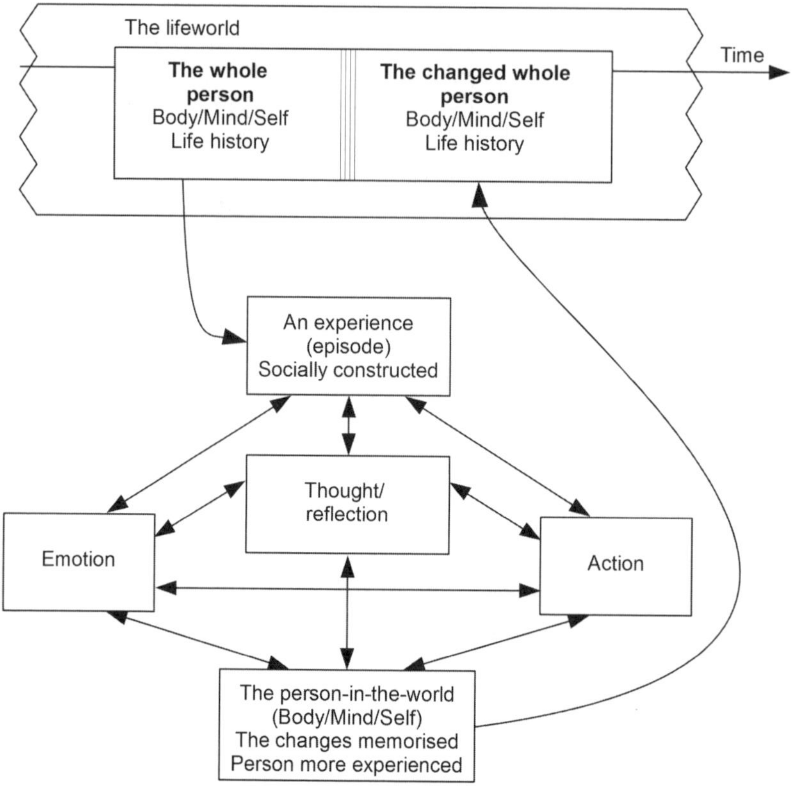

Source: Jarvis, 2006, p. 23

With this model, Jarvis joins those theorists who emphasise that learning is a transformative process, even though his concept of transformation is a bit different than Mezirow's, for example. Whereas the latter sees transformational learning as a particular type of learning (see Chapter 2.2), Jarvis thinks of *any* kind of learning as a process that involves changing as a person, and therefore as a transformative incident. Again, it is the person that is at the core of his interest in learning.

Although Jarvis designed the model depicted in Figure 7 as a follow-up to his earlier approaches, its potentiality to deliver a better description of adult learning processes seems doubtful. We do not have to regard it as rivalling earlier approaches, however. Rather, the model in Figure 7 shows a person-centred concept of learning in which the change of the person is predominant, and in which other aspects of the learning process are subordinated to that particular perspective. Whereas the concept of transformational learning considers the transformation of the person to be part of the learning process, Jarvis's model takes the opposite approach by describing the learning process as a particular type of personal change. With that in mind, Jarvis delivers a complimentary look on learning rather than an alternative.

His concept of learning is rather precise, especially with respect to the definition quoted above. It describes learning as the change of the person. On other occasions, he situated this change within the lifeworld (cf. Jarvis, 2006, pp. 194ff.). In a more recent book (Jarvis, 2009), he explored these ideas in more detail, partly returning to a sociological point of view and further investigating social perspectives such as interaction. These conceptions are of particular importance when learning is defined as a 'change of the person in the world' (Pätzold, 2008). This perspective leads to three crucial characteristics of a comprehensive pedagogical concept of learning:

- Learning is change. Therefore, it is a process to be observed *in time*. Theoretical and empirical concepts of learning have to construct some virtual or real difference between a *status quo ante* and a *status quo post* in the experience of learning (see also Chapter 9.1).
- At the core of learning is the *person*. Learning theory must consider all aspects of the person, including mind and body, and must not neglect any aspects of this unity. Eventually, this leads to the phenomenological perspective referred to as the *lived body* (see also Chapter 9.2).
- Learning is situated in the *world* – again conceived as a unity of what is given materially and what is experienced mentally or socially. Therefore, learning always has to do with a relationship between the person and the

world. From a phenomenological point of view, this leads to the idea of the lifeworld (see also Chapter 9.3).

We will come back to those three issues in Part Two, when discussing their consequences for didactics. Before doing so, we should assess Jarvis's concept a little further. Though doubtlessly an important contribution to the theory of adult learning, it still leaves some questions for further research. First, the empirical basis is rather weak. In contrast to concepts such as phenomenography (see Chapter 3.1), which involve a comprehensive theory as well as detailed and diligent empirical studies, Jarvis's theory of human learning is more suitable for contributing to the 'big picture'. His research approach has proved fruitful for exploring an individual's perspectives on learning, but it is not (and was not meant to be) sufficient for providing an in-depth analysis of general processes of human learning. This also holds for the various learning paths that Jarvis has discussed against this background (Jarvis, 2006, pp. 10ff.). They may often be seen as inspiring metaphors, but we should not expect them to form a comprehensive system of possible learning paths.

The second model, shown in Figure 7, provides a more or less metatheoretical perspective. The concept of the person can be exploited to enrich pedagogical learning theory, but it itself lacks a systematic framework of reference within or outside educational science. Yet it may serve well as a background for interpretation, when relations between learning and lifeworld are discussed, for example.

In his ongoing work, Jarvis keeps creating an often inspiring and sometimes surprising mix of contributions to learning theory. His thinking draws on a diverse range of sources including philosophy (ranging from Confucius through Husserl to Foucault), psychology (with an emphasis on Piaget, but further references to Freud, Dewey, and many others), and a variety of other references. His early work in particular was so strongly related to symbolic interactionism that it was regarded as the 'translation of symbolic interactionism into a model of adult learning' (Finger & Asún, 2001, p. 51). More recent publications feature strong links to phenomenology, adding yet another perspective to Jarvis's thinking.

Jarvis obviously doesn't aim to literally bind all those contributions together to form a consistent and comprehensive theory; instead, he uses them as a repository of inspiring thoughts on the overall topic. In doing so, he provides a unique body of work that raises our awareness of the connections between different theoretical perspectives on learning, thereby creating a kind of network of ideas without sticking to one particular school of thought.

However, two of these schools are so important and had such a strong impact (not just on Jarvis's thinking) that they deserve to be discussed in this study guide.

5.2 Humanism and pragmatism: The roots and branches of modern learning theory?

In 2001, Matthias Finger and Jóse Manuel Asún wrote that adult education is at a crossroads. Over the past couple of decades, it has increasingly evolved into a support structure for the (mainly industrial) development of societies and economies. Although this implies great success in terms of scope and impact and has led to numerous positive developments (e.g. increasing the number of adult education providers, establishing structures of public funding for adult education, recognising adult education as an academic subject, etc.), it may still turn out to be a dead end. Finger and Asún fear that, strangled by its own success, adult education may grow out of touch with its roots and traditions, particularly the ethical agenda it once started out with. They refer to Ivan Illich, the great educational thinker (and doer) from Latin America, who became aware of this danger early on:

More than ever before, his thinking is relevant today, as the very idea of 'sustainable' industrial development goes up in smoke, while all its sustaining institutions try to survive ... and make things worse in doing so. (Finger & Asún, 2001, p. 3)

Echoing Illich's warning, Finger and Asún aim to bring adult education back in line with the unique contribution it can make to society as long as it is not co-opted by particular institutions, sectors, or interests. To help adult education return to its fundamental traditions, they identify two main roots of adult education philosophy, which they believe may serve as pivotal streams of thinking: humanism and pragmatism. The following sections are loosely based on their enthusiastic praise of these two schools of thought. To Finger and Asún, pragmatism is a 'genuine American highway' (ibid., p. 29), and humanism no less than a 'lonely traveller on the road to heaven' (ibid., p. 62). Both philosophies have in common that they – unlike the majority of contemporary contributions to educational philosophy – are based on a particular set of anthropological assumptions about humans as learners that lie beneath their practical conclusions.

It is a popular misunderstanding to regard 'pragmatic action' as action without theory. What the pragmatic approach opposes, however, is theory without action. With its popular claim that 'truth is what works' (Skirbekk & Gilje, 2001, p. 362), pragmatism is related both to behaviourism and to a certain understanding of constructivism. However, pragmatism also has a challenging moral background. John Dewey, one of the foremost representatives of this educational and philosophical paradigm, is acknowledged as a relentless advocate of democracy, and one of his most famous books is devoted to the relationship between democracy and education (Dewey, 1916). Other representatives of pragmatism include Eduard Lindemann and William James.

Figure 8: A learning cycle according to John Dewey; for an alternative suggestion, review Kolb's model in Figure 5

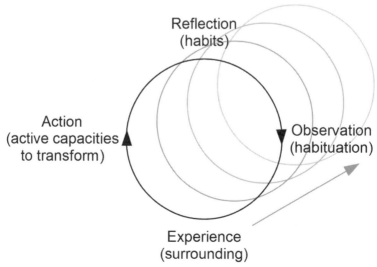

Source: Finger & Asún, 2001, p. 33

According to Dewey, learning is part of a larger process of growth, which is an intrinsic human potentiality. Humans are characterised by their ability to use language and to learn from previous experience (and, moreover, to build on this learning and thereby reach higher levels of both individual and social development). Therefore, while also serving social and economic needs, learning in its essence shall contribute to humanisation and progress. In a learning cycle based on Dewey's philosophy, humans are habitualised (socialised) to their environment because of their prior experience. This habituation produces habits (social beliefs, norms, values, and cultures). These habits in turn lead to new actions that bring about new experiences, thereby allowing the process to continue indefinitely (see Figure 8).

Dewey's philosophy draws our attention to the close link between learning and culture. As learning requires a stepwise process of leaving dysfunctional habits behind and developing new ones, rigid societies often obstruct further development at both the social and the individual levels. Likewise, orienting education merely towards economic goals imposes too many limits on open development. Accordingly, education serves three main purposes:

- It prepares individuals for finding their place and getting involved in the society they live in.
- It creates and maintains a potentiality to foster innovation and creativity (including innovations to change society).
- It is action in and of itself, designed to help the individual and society in general evolve and, specifically, to enhance their problem-solving ability.

From this point of view, education is a core process for maintaining and developing society itself. It can only be used to support social development, however, not to shape it or to give it a particular direction. As innovation and problem-solving potential refer to yet unknown future situations and abilities, their content cannot be foreseen. As a consequence, they cannot be anticipated in curricula, fixed programmes of adult education, or similar steering measures.

Another important aspect of Dewey's approach (and of pragmatism in general) is his emphasis on experience. Individual learning is based on the reflection of experience and the corresponding action. Similarly, learning in societies must be open to collective endeavour to minimise the danger of subjectivity in reflection. Individual learners need the collective as a source of experience in a way that allows them to change their concepts, beliefs, and convictions. Experience does not necessarily mean the complete failure of such a concept; rather, learners may experiment with it by engaging in a collective discussion before actually putting it to practice.

With respect to the philosophies presented thus far, pragmatism serves as a link between quite different strands of theory. Not only does it connect behaviourism and constructivism, it also has much in common with other concepts mentioned here. Both Dewey and Jarvis, for example, focus on the individual, defined as a person in society (cf. Jarvis, 2009). Dewey put experience at the centre of his learning theory, as did many others afterwards. And despite his practical approach, Dewey never lost sight of the moral foundations of education. At this point, it even seems doubtful whether it is wise to follow Finger and Asún in their distinction between pragmatist and humanist approaches towards adult education. As pragmatist thought is based on an anthropology that clearly regards humans as social beings with a certain urge to grow and develop, it may be seen as closely akin to humanist theory in a certain sense. These similarities notwithstanding, humanist theory is also remarkably different from pragmatism, both regarding its core ideas and its main representatives.

Keyword: Humanism

The origins of humanism go far back in history. Originally, the term referred to the historical period that followed the Middle Ages and ushered in modernity (Rabil, n.d.). Humanist philosophers such as Petrarch or Erasmus of Rotterdam revived ancient Greek and Roman thought, proclaiming the ideal of universal education and knowledge, and generally placed human beings at the centre of all philosophical consideration.

The work of humanist philosophers was devoted to improving people's historical and social conditions and to promoting the free development of creative and constructive human powers. Humanist thinking in the modern social sciences, particularly in education and psychology, has reflected this period in various ways. In the eighteenth century, with the German discourse on *Bildung* in full swing, Wilhelm von Humboldt referred to humanist thinking when championing the idea of a well-rounded education and defending it against those who saw schooling and education as a merely utilitarian enterprise to produce students that satisfied certain social or economic demands. He thereby fostered the idea of a general type of learning, one that was not tied to specific uses and applications (which is why Humboldt may be regarded as an early advocate of the concept of key competencies). As Humboldt and others referred to the humanist philosophers, their approach is sometimes called *neo-humanism*.

In the mid-twentieth century, the term *humanistic* was applied to a variety of mainly psychological approaches that were more or less based on the work of Carl Ransom Rogers. (Other representatives include Abraham Maslow, Erich Fromm, and Ruth Cohn, for example.) Like pragmatism, humanistic psychology endorses a particular perspective on humans that, according to Rogers, can be summarised in three main assumptions (cf. Finger & Asún 2001, pp. 58ff.; see also Bélanger, 2011):

- Human beings are active, free, and good.
- Humans have an intrinsic motivation to develop.
- Whether humans activate and realise their urge to develop is deeply influenced by their material and social circumstances.

Despite reports to the contrary, the humanistic position is not merely a naïve belief in the goodness of every human being. Rogers and many other representatives of humanistic psychology were practising psychotherapists and knew quite a bit about the abysses of human nature. Yet they were convinced that it was misleading to regard these dark sides as 'normal'; instead, psychology and psychotherapy should strive to (re-)activate the potentialities named above.

Although the founders of this branch of humanism were psychologists, there soon was a growing number of contributions from education, not least because many of the humanistic psychologists were quite interested in educational questions. The posited process of individual development and growth has so much in common with concepts of learning that it cannot be easily distinguished from change processes restricted to therapeutic intervention. Regers himself said the difference between the two was merely a matter of the context in which they occur. In other words, the core ideas of humanistic psychology can be transferred to humanistic education mostly without alterations. More specifically, both rely on 'human-centeredness, a sense of personal autonomy, the idea of human dignity, the principle of virtuous action, and a sense of personal responsibility' (Pearson & Podeschi, 1999, pp. 43–44).

It is not surprising, therefore, that the humanistic approach was quite popular in education. Part of its attractiveness lies in the fact that it provides a positive view of humans while still offering concrete approaches for intervention. Most importantly, it regards learning as something that humans generally do not have to be forced to do – instead, there is a natural urge to learn which only needs to be channelled into the desired direction. To be sure, humanistic education theory has also drawn a lot of criticism, mainly regarding the lack of empirical evidence for large parts of the concept (even though this is a typical feature of a considerable number of theories of that time). Some fundamental concepts of humanistic psychology, including such popular ideas as Maslow's hierarchy of needs, still lack proof in terms of empirical research.

Then again, many humanistic beliefs lately seem to be validated in other ways, for example by findings in neuroscience. The importance of emotions, for example, not only with regard to motivation but also with regard to actual learning outcomes, was highlighted in the humanistic concept and has been confirmed through a variety of alternative efforts in learning research. The general approach of self-directedness in learning has also gained significant importance in both research and practice. Admittedly, there are no simple and superior humanistic didactic arrangements – but then again, even behaviourists, with their vast body of empirical evidence, cannot claim to have devised such general methods or settings.

The idea of self-directedness in learning is one of the key contributions of humanistic psychology to education. For instance, it has become an essential component in the American approach of *andragogy* (Knowles, 1975; Knowles, Holton, & Swanson, 2005).

Keyword: Andragogy

Perpetuating the idea of human centring, andragogy focuses on learning as a fundamentally individualised process that may be 'facilitated', to use one of Rogers's terms, rather than 'conducted' through teaching. Self-directed learning means that learners are autonomous throughout the whole process of controlling their learning (without necessarily refusing help from others). Thus humanism, on the one hand, contributes to a particular understanding of learning as a self-logical process; on the other hand, like pragmatism, it addresses an ethical dimension in basing any individual learning effort on the strife for growth and development.

What pragmatism and humanism have in common is the proposition that learning is more than a means to a certain end; rather, it is a manifestation of humanity itself. Whereas pragmatism emphasises the social dimension (learning prepares individuals for finding their place and getting involved in society), humanism emphasises the individual dimension (learning is, first and foremost, a necessary means to preventing the individual from being exploited by society). Both concepts further share the idea of learning as a process related to persons. It would not be possible, therefore, to formulate a theory of learning organisations or machines in line with the original concepts of pragmatist or humanist learning. (Modern theories on learning organisations *refer* to those concepts, of course, but they would not simply *transfer* them.) Moreover, by proposing specific ideas about learning, both pragmatism and humanism have at least partly similar consequences for teaching. Pragmatism emphasises the importance of experience, but humanistic learning can hardly be imagined without experience either, especially because the teacher's role is that of a facilitator. Accordingly, both theories would claim that learning, at least to a certain extent, relies on a social counterpart. Finally, both theories suggest that the outcomes of learning cannot and should not be systematically determined in advance, because this would contradict the general openness of the process. Looking at the differences between the two approaches, we see that pragmatism has more of a social perspective whereas humanism is more concerned with the individual. Accordingly, pragmatism tends to place more emphasis on the measurable results of learning, whereas humanism tends to leave this assessment to the individual and therefore is less suitable for traditional empirical research.

Humanism and pragmatism belong to the very foundations of modern thinking in adult education. Their impact on adult education theory continues to today, and both philosophies are revisited on a regular basis every time new findings in educational science and neighbouring disciplines emerge. They may very well be regarded as the roots of contemporary adult education theory, because in contrast to the sociological 'classics' (such as Foucault or Bourdieu, for example), they have something more particular to say about individual learning. Yet they also provide an anthropological and ethical dimension, which is often absent in modern discussions on learning, teaching, and adult education in general. While seeking to create a thorough picture of what constitutes learning, they do not lose sight of the theoretical foundations from which they started: learning as a change process of societies and individuals. This perspective eventually calls for ideas about what these processes may lead to. Ultimately, such ideas cannot escape being influenced by normative positions, a fact that humanism and pragmatism do not deny. Contemporary contributions to learning theory, and even more to teaching methodology, should be aware that from a certain stage onwards, it is necessary to use *and* reflect upon their underlying normative presumptions. The presumptions of humanism and pragmatism are certainly not the only ones out there, but they may serve to remind us of the necessity of normative reflection. Therefore, humanism and pragmatism may not only be regarded as roots but also as branches of modern learning theory.

Exercises and tasks

Exercise 1

Use Kolb's learning cycle as a starting point to design your own concept of learning. Change phases, lines, and arrows to create a model that seems appropriate for describing the diversity of your own learning processes. At the same time, be careful not to make the model too abstract.

Exercise 2

Think about other schools of philosophy besides humanism and pragmatism. Is there something you might want to consider from a philosophical point of view when thinking about learning?

Task 1

Use Internet resources to find out about Kolb's 'learning style inventory'. Look at the corresponding tests and maybe try them yourself. Discuss the concept (and the test results) with respect to your own ideas about (your own) learning. The following links are online adaptations of the Learning Style Inventory. Please keep in mind that they are only intended to give an impression of Kolb's original work.

http://www.nwlink.com/~donclark/hrd/styles/learn_style_survey.html

http://www.cadplan.com.au/KolbOnline.html

Task 2

If you explored Kolb's learning style inventory (Task 1), you will have encountered the terms *accommodator* and *assimilator*. Find out about Piaget's idea of those two terms.

Task 3

When discussing the work of Peter Jarvis, we referred to Robert Merton's term *middle range theory*. What did Merton himself mean by it? Have a look at Merton (1957) and discuss whether the middle range approach is appropriate for a theory of adult learning, or whether adult learning deserves a broader (or narrower) theoretical approach.

Merton, R. (1957). The role-set: Problems in sociological theory. *British Journal of Sociology*, 8(2), 106–120. Retrieved from http://www.jstor.org/stable/587363?seq=2.

6. Looking Beyond One's Own Nose: Psychological Approaches and Neurosciences

6.1 A brief glance at behaviourism, cognitivism, and constructivism

In most books about learning theory or educational psychology, readers sooner or later encounter well-known terms such as behaviourism, cognitivism, constructivism, and so forth. For a long time, these approaches, in their attempt to capture a virtually invisible process, have served as a kind of para-mechanical theory of the learning process itself. Although human learning can never be observed directly – we can see a change in somebody's behaviour, but we usually cannot be sure about the reason for this change – these approaches were models for describing either the 'phenomenological' (behaviourism) or the 'internal' (cognitivism, constructivism) aspects of the process.

Behaviourism, for example, describes *mechanisms* of learning basically as building up chains of stimulus and response. In doing so, the theory provides a model for predicting the outcome of a certain treatment towards a learning entity, usually a human being or an animal. Combining, for example, an aversive stimulus with a neutral one will, after a while, usually result in avoidance as a reaction to the formerly neutral stimulus. Yet the model becomes increasingly complicated when it comes to those kinds of learning processes that involve learning a complex matter by rather indirect action (such as discussion, observation, modelling, etc.) or learning something new all at once – that is, without a repeated sequence of stimuli and responses. The former problem in particular is caused by an a priori theoretical decision that initially contributed much to the success of behaviourism: the decision to disregard the cognitive system itself. The famous term *black box* is a metaphor for the inaccessibility of a cognitive system, even though early behaviourists seem not to have used the term themselves.

> **Keyword: Black Box**
>
> The term *black box* refers to an entity which can be examined only indirectly by providing certain inputs and evaluating the output. By means of experiment and observation, one may find out *what* a black box does (i.e. what kind of reaction it shows to a certain input under certain circumstances). Its inner workings, however, are inaccessible – that is, *how* the black box works is mere speculation.

As internal states are not accessible, learning by talking is generally difficult to capture. Discussions about how somebody 'feels' when 'experiencing' this or that, or about the 'judgements' this person would eventually make, is basically talk about internal states and – although it obviously may be part of a learning process – quite difficult to deal with in behaviouristic terms. Behaviourists therefore, instead of claiming direct access to people's thoughts, beliefs, and so on, insist that we draw conclusions exclusively from observing someone's behaviour. This assumption proved fruitful during the development of behaviourism, but it later turned out to be an obstacle, as seen above.

Although researchers generally agree that internal conditions (such as motivation, lust, etc.) cannot be observed directly, it still seems necessary to assume the existence of these conditions to gain an understanding of learning, defined as a change in behaviour. This is why cognitivism eventually ended the hegemony of behaviourism as a dominant school of thought in psychology. To a great extent, this is owed to the inspiring pioneer work of the Swiss psychologist and development theorist Jean Piaget. In contrast to the behaviourists, Piaget formed a sophisticated system of central internal concepts and developed creative and demonstrative experiments to find out when and how these concepts are formed by children. A prominent example is the concept of *object permanence*. Piaget stated that toddlers at the age of about ten months start to realise that objects do not just disappear when they are out of sight, but stay in (invisible) existence. From this moment onwards, much to many parents' dismay, it is no longer possible to distract a child's attention from some object just by covering it. Though the respective behaviour (e.g. searching for the object) is observable, the concept of object permanence itself is not. Whereas behaviourism basically aims to provide a kind of model for predicting behaviour, cognitivism seeks to find theoretical explanations for why particular learning tasks can be accomplished (whereas others cannot). Furthermore, it ties those explanations to the developmental stage an individual is in. Therefore, cognitivism also directs our attention to the ways in which learning processes change throughout an individual's development.

Figure 9: A schematic comparison of behaviourism and cognitivism

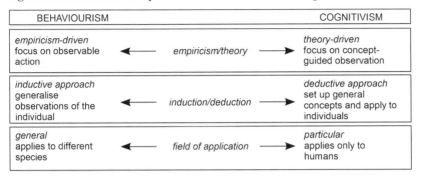

Source: own source

Figure 9 compares both strands of thought in a rather broad-brush manner, pointing out their differences in emphasis while also showing a considerable degree of overlap in each of the three dimensions indicated in the figure. Yet we can see that the approach of behaviourism is *more* on the inductive side, *more* related to empirical research, and of *greater* generality than cognitivism. Compared to behaviourism, cognitivism provides a more sophisticated theory and more details about human learning in particular. This explains an important observation concerning practitioners who deal with both theories. Whereas the theoretical assumptions are quite different and can barely be harmonised, the two theories may very well be applied in combination in practical situations. We may often find a practitioner explaining one part of a learner's behaviour in behaviourist terms and another in cognitivist terms – as in the statement, 'Because of the positive feedback she received, she made even more of an effort; now she finally understood the issue.' Whereas the first part refers to an observable positive stimulus and its consequence (and thus to behaviour), the second deals with the internal concept of understanding something. Yet once again, the stimulus itself, positive feedback, can hardly be understood without referring to inner states. So despite their profound differences in theory, cognitivism and behaviourism merely seem to look at the same subject from different angles. Both approaches try to contribute to a theoretical framework of 'mechanisms' that lie beneath the process of learning.

Whereas behaviourism and cognitivism are both firmly rooted in the history of psychology, constructivism, a third major branch of learning theory, evolved out of sociology, biology, cybernetics, and other disciplines. Taken together, the various contributions from these fields form the family of constructivist approaches: social constructivism (cf. Berger & Luckmann, 1966), radical constructivism (cf. von Glasersfeld, 1995), or other branches of systemic-constructivist thinking (cf. Arnold, 2005, pp. 65–66). All of them have in common that they regard somebody's world view as an individual construction resulting from the internal processing of information – a point of view they more or less share with cognitivism. (Glasersfeld in particular based a good deal of his own thinking on the work of Piaget.) Yet whereas cognitivism emphasises the mutual patterns of learning and development, constructivism seeks to shed light on the question why, in spite of the inevitable individual *differences* in constructing a world view, we end up with the impression that other people's conceptions of the world seem to be quite similar to our own. This is expressed in the fact that constructivism is often regarded as an epistemology (and therefore as being closer to the individual's cognisance), whereas cognitivism is related to development, emphasising general patterns above and beyond the individual. This has consequences for the whole scientific approach underlying the concept of learning and the related research. The fact that constructivists, and radical constructivists in particular, are quite reluctant to accept that any kind of objective, material outer world exists leads to significant differences in the way they address the phenomenon of learning. Whereas behaviourism and cognitivism differ only in the weight they put on empiricism or theory, constructivism essentially calls for an alternative philosophy of science. Accordingly, the terms *induction* and *deduction* hardly apply, because both of these principles are based on some kind of generally valid truth. Consequently, the generality of the field of application, which started to decrease from behaviourism to cognitivism, is now lost completely: radical constructivist statements cannot be generalised in any reliable way. The challenges of formulating a theory of learning according to radical constructivism are shown in Figure 10.

While the challenges of (radical) constructivism to the traditional philosophy of science shall not be denied, more moderate strands of constructivist thinking have already had a profound impact on pedagogy, both with regard to the theory of learning and a wide range of didactic considerations, mainly in the field of media education.

Overall, the psychological approaches (and constructivism as a related one) seek to explain the general processes that underlie learning. In this respect, they are comparable to the natural sciences, which try to reveal the natural laws that form the basis of physical, chemical, or biological occurrences. Education researchers sometimes use the respective results in the same way that engineers exploit findings from physics: to develop, try out, or justify specific concepts, treatments, and the like. For a long time, it seemed that the natural sciences on the one hand and the 'mind sciences' on the other could not become more equivalent, as there was no hint that it may be possible to deal with mental phenomena in a way similar to the way natural sciences treat material phenomena. In recent decades, however, that expectation has been disproved by the immense progress made in the field of neuroscience within a short period of time. The following section provides an introduction to neuroscience and its implications for learning theory.

Figure 10: A comparison between cognitivism/behaviourism and constructivism

BEHAVIOURISM	COGNITIVISM		CONSTRUCTIVISM
empiricism-driven *focus on observable* *action*	*theory-driven* *focus on concept- guided observation*	*empiricism/ theory*	*demanding a new philosophy of science including concepts of theory and empiricism*
inductive approach *generalise observations of the individual*	*deductive approach* *set up general concepts and apply to individuals*	*induction/ deduction*	*not applicable in a strict sense*
general *applies to different species*	*particular* *applies only to humans*	*field of application*	*application is essentially restricted to the single individual*

Source: own source

6.2 The learning brain?

The basic concepts of behaviourism entered the field of learning and teaching at a time of great expectations and optimism that bordered on fantasies of omnipotence. One of the immediate visible results was the creation of a concept called *programmed instruction* in the late 1950s (cf. Bullock, 1978). As behaviourists succeeded in teaching animals to perform rather complex actions by cueing them in a series of stimuli-response-frames, it seemed promising to transfer this approach to human learners and find an efficient and reliable way of teaching virtually anything to anybody. It seemed that the very laws of learning had been revealed and were now at hand to revolutionise learning and teaching. History has proven this expectation wrong: some of the seemingly new insights were already widely used by practitioners (like enforcing desired behaviour), others were applicable only within a limited area. Gradually, expectations were reduced, and eventually behaviourism found its place among other approaches in learning theory and didactics. Surprisingly, the picture seems quite similar when we look at today's progress in neuroscience. There are loads of articles and books promising a revolution once again, this time based on findings in the brain, the material apparatus of thinking. Level-headed commentators, however, keep advising against simplifying applications of the results from neuroscience. Cognitive neuroscience – the combined study of cognitive processes, the human brain, and neuronal structures –

is an exciting and new scientific endeavour, but it is also a very young one. As a result we know relatively little about learning, thinking, and remembering at the level of brain areas, neural circuits, or synapses; we know very little about how the brain thinks, remembers, and learns. (Bruer, 2008, p. 53)

Bruer convincingly calls for restraint in putting neuroscience knowledge into practice, and yet there are a number of conclusions to be drawn from recent developments in this area with respect to the theory of learning and teaching. There is no reason to reduce our concepts of mental processes to what can be explained by the underlying neuronal activity; however, neither must we ignore the existing knowledge of the material side of mental activity. From the various examples of what neuronal processes and structures may have to do with learning, the discussion on mirror neurons shall be presented in a little more detail. Basically, mirror neurons are a specific type of nerve cell that shows activity when somebody observes a certain action, image, and so on. The crucial point is that they do not reside in those areas of the brain where the corresponding actions or images are expected to be perceived; instead, they are found in those areas that are used to *perform* an action or produce a feeling similar to the one observed.

Up until now, the majority of research in this area has been done on motor mirror neurons. They happen to show activity when we observe someone else perform an action that we could have also performed ourselves. In animal experiments, it has been shown that a monkey's mirror neurons are active when it observes another monkey grasping a peanut. Again, the important detail here is that those neurons are located in the motor area of the monkey's brain; that is to say, the same neurons are active when the monkey itself grasps a peanut. They are the first neurons to be discovered in the motor area that participate in a process of recognition. Moreover, if the monkey observes the same movement as before, but without the peanut being there to grasp, the neurons stay silent. It seems that those mirror neurons are realising the aim of a particular movement in a pre-conscious way (cf. Rizzolatti & Sinigaglia, 2008; Pätzold, 2010a). They form a structure that allows us to understand somebody else's action by experiencing a kind of internal resonance along with what is observed outside. Vittorio Gallese, one of the researchers who originally discovered mirror neurons, uses the term 'embodied simulation' (Gallese, 2005) to describe their function: 'Our brains, and those of other primates, appear to have developed a basic functional mechanism, embodied simulation, which gives us an experiential insight of other minds.' (Gallese et al., 2004, p. 401)

Mirror neurons do not only exist in motor areas of the brain, however; ongoing research has discovered several other areas and types of mirror neurons. It seems that mirror neuron clusters are also involved in understanding other people's emotions (cf. Gallese, 2005, p. 37). Furthermore, there are 'audiovisual mirror neurons' (ibid.) linking auditive and visual experiences. The whole system of mirror neurons supports mutual understanding on different levels, from observing and understanding actions to empathising with others. The simulative character of the mirror neuron system is also described by the term *resonance*. Observing a particular action may lead to resonance within the observer, and this resonance helps the observer understand what he or she observed. Consequently, the degree of resonance with respect to a certain observation may vary between different observers. The term resonance was originally used to describe an acoustic phenomenon. A relatively small amount of energy can cause vibrations in an oscillatory system if the frequency of the impulse is similar to the eigenfrequency of the system. For instance, a sound may cause a guitar string to oscillate if it is of the same pitch the string is tuned to. Similarly, the metaphor of tuning is used in descriptions of mirror neurons. We may experience resonance within our mirror neuron system if we are 'tuned' accordingly Gallese uses the term *intentional attunement* (Gallese, 2005, p. 31) to make clear that this tuning is not a fixed bodily characteristic but something which can be changed and developed.

It is quite obvious that these findings may have an impact on our ideas of learning and teaching. Learning specific movements (e.g. in physical training) seems to depend on prior conceptual insights into the *whole movement*: therefore, it might in some cases be counterproductive to decompose movements into smaller, seemingly easier parts to facilitate learning. Moreover, the concept of intentional attunement clearly shows that learning specific emotional and social actions might be eased by learning more about the process of attunement. Eventually, the respective processes may be harnessed to benefit teaching.

The findings on mirror neurons – as well as similar results of recent neuroscience – promise to give us a significantly deeper insight into the neuronal processes that go along with learning, but they must not be confused with the phenomenon itself. From a pedagogical perspective, it is not the brain that learns, but the person: anybody who works in the field of education is involved with persons, after all, not with brains (Jarvis, 2006; Giesinger, 2006; Meyer-Drawe, 2008).

6.3 Conclusions

The term *learning* is not so clear once we look at its meanings in different contexts. In addition to the various actors (people, cognitive systems, brains, etc.) that are regarded as learners in the discussions mentioned above, we also talk about learning organisations, companies, and even immune systems. It seems necessary, therefore, to further clarify the concept of learning we wish to adhere to in pedagogical contexts. Again, the reference shall be the person, understood mainly in phenomenological terms. Based on this qualification, the contributions of other sciences can be ordered accordingly without competing with one another.

- *Behaviourism* (including both the classic concepts and more elaborated recent contributions to psychology known as behavioural science) captures learning as causing changes in behaviour. More precisely, as the research focus of behaviourism is on predicting those changes according to specific interventions, learning causes predicable changes in behaviour. To study learning in a behaviourist manner therefore means first of all to see the subject as a learning system in a behaviourist sense. This is by no means a weakness of the theory, but it has to be kept in mind when applying behaviourist findings to educational situations. When doing so, one has to first make clear that the view of the subjects (usually the learners) can safely be reduced to learning systems in the abovementioned sense. From this perspective, behaviourist learning theory may fruitfully explain *aspects* of learning – particularly those aspects that can be organised according to the basic principles of stimulus and response – without claiming to be a general theory of learning in educational situations.
- *Cognitivism* amends the behaviourist approach by addressing internal states of the learning subject. One consequence of this change in focus is that cognitivism can be applied only to human learning (as the opportunities to gain reliable assertions about internal states of other beings are very limited). Obviously, this is not a serious constraint with respect to

pedagogy. However, the cognitivist approach also carries another limitation in its understanding of learning as first and foremost a cognitive process. Cognitive aspects doubtlessly play an important role in learning, but there are other dimensions that might be neglected this way. To begin with, a naïve cognitivist would most likely underestimate the importance of emotions. But even if emotions are taken into account, there are still other relevant aspects to be considered. They may be captured by the phenomenological term of the *lived body* (*Leib* in German, Colombetti & Thompson, 2007, p. 57). That said, cognitivism has a lot to say about the cognitive aspects of learning. Its insights into the development of certain concepts of thinking in particular are of great value. Piaget and his vast array of successors have found out striking details about learning in a diverse range of subjects including numbers, geometry, morale, and many others. Cognitivism thus provides another piece to the jigsaw puzzle of learning, but like behaviourism, it cannot claim to be a comprehensive theory of learning.

- *Constructivism* in a way grew out of the combination of cognitivist thinking and other, particularly systemic, thoughts. It is sometimes regarded as a learning theory in its own right, but its original aspiration reaches further, questioning the very basics of the philosophy of science. Then again, constructivism lately has produced a variety of new contributions to teaching methodology, and, furthermore, has been utilised to justify and refine existing ones. Constructivism therefore has already proven to be an inspiring model of learning and may very well stimulate creative didactic thinking. Yet to serve as a learning theory, it still lacks fundamental theoretical clarifications (e.g. concerning the actor who is actually doing the constructing). In its more moderate, education-related variants, constructivism usually shares the cognitive bias of cognitivism, its psychological root. In our discussions of learning and teaching, constructivism is useful for showing the opportunities as well as the pitfalls to be aware of when going from theory to practice in the field of learning and teaching.

- *Neuroscience* turns out to be a rich source of inspiration for educational thinking on learning and teaching. Not only do some of its recent findings provide empirical evidence to support existing pedagogic convictions (and disprove some other cherished beliefs), its new insights into the brain's function may also guide us towards answers to open questions within existing theories of mental processes. Mirror neurons, for example, may explain the convergence of experience between different individuals, which is still quite mysterious from a radical constructivist's point of view. From a pedagogic point of view, however, we need to make clear that neuroscience is limited to those aspects of learning that are related more or less directly to neural processes. As with cognitivism, there is no doubt about the general importance of neural activity in learning, but neuroscience, with its restricted focus on this activity, positively cannot cover the phenomenon of learning in its entirety.

The role that psychological and biological concepts of learning play in the debate on education in general and on adult education in particular cannot easily be underestimated. Any educational professional is expected to know about the fundamental mechanisms of cognitive processes, and especially about their implications for learning. When planning educational interventions of any sort, he or she should be aware of what those theories might contribute to the design of those plans and to the evaluation of outcomes. Therefore, students in adult education are strongly encouraged to explore these psychological and biological concepts in more detail than can be provided in this study guide (see e.g. Bélanger, 2011, for an expanded presentation of psychological theories). Authors such as Jarvis (2006, pp.177ff.) or Gieseke (2007, pp. 49ff.) extensively discuss the respective findings in psychology, neuroscience, emotional psychology, and so forth. On the other hand, the overview of theories presented in this chapter was also meant to illustrate the limitations of approaches towards learning that were imported from other disciplines. Although it is absolutely necessary to know and utilise them, they cannot replace concepts rooted in educational science to capture the phenomenon of learning from a pedagogic perspective. Johann Friedrich Herbart, the German philosopher and psychologist who founded pedagogy as an academic discipline, once claimed that pedagogy has to rely on 'native terms' (Herbart, 1806/1992). Although the term *learning* is used in a variety of disciplines ranging from medicine to education, management, and cybernetics, it is reasonable, from my point of view, to treat it as a term native to education – that is to say, to *relate* it to the meanings it receives in other disciplines rather than to *replace* it with those other meanings.

Exercises and tasks

Exercise 1

Think of a particular subject matter in adult education. Which didactic decisions do you think might be particularly promising in a learning situation if you wanted to account for the alleged functions of mirror neurons in your actions?

Exercise 2

The authors of some recent books and articles talk about the 'learning brain', or use similar phrases. Relate this usage of the term *learning* to the way the term is used in previous chapters of this study guide.

Task 1

Have a look at the volume by Paul Bélanger (2011) in this study guide series (see below). If we keep thinking of learning as *a change of the person in the lifeworld* – how does this change primarily take place, according to each of the three main theories described in Part 1 of Bélanger's book?

Bélanger, P. (2011). *Theories in adult learning and education.* Opladen: Budrich.

Task 2

We frequently mentioned the idea of *learning as a change of the person.* Compare this concept of the person to that used in neurosciences, particularly with respect to the mirror neurons.

Gallese, V., Eagle, M. N. & Migone, P. (2007). Intentional attunement: Mirror neurons and the neural underpinnings of interpersonal relations. *Journal of the American Psychoanalytical Association*, 55(1), 132–176.

Part Two
The 'Art of Teaching':
Exploring Concepts of Adult
Learning to Address Didactic
Challenges

7. Didactics and Didactic Models

7.1 Preliminaries on the term *didactic*

The term *didactic* is used quite often in this study guide. But even though it is a common word in many European languages, its meanings vary significantly. Moreover, even within one single language, the term may not always mean exactly the same. In this book, *didactic* will be used to describe the thoughts and actions of people professionally involved in the field of education. This covers teaching, training, and facilitating, as well as planning and evaluation. Since this is not a universally accepted definition, it shall be justified (and specified further) with the help of some brief historical and terminological remarks.

The origin of the term *didactic* (from Greek *didaktikos*, from *didaskein* 'teach') may be traced to John Amos Comenius's *Didactica Magna*. Originally published in Latin in 1657, it is considered to be the first major book on pedagogy generally. Comenius used the term *didactic* to provide a general method or, more precisely, a pathway to overcome the shortcomings of all prior attempts of schooling and teaching. Right in the first chapter, he formulated his ambitious claim:

We venture to promise a GREAT DIDACTIC, that is to say, the whole art of teaching all things to all men, and indeed of teaching them with certainty, so that the result cannot fail to follow. (Comenius, 1657/1967, p. 5)

With this statement, Comenius probably prepared the ground both for the term's successful career and for the continuous debate about it. On the one hand, he stated that didactics was the right term to address the effort of *teaching professionally and appropriately,* which in fact means that teaching should first and foremost serve the well-being of the individual. (Comenius assumed that educators would be guided by a well-understood Christian world view.) On the other hand, he also stated that there could be some *infallible pathway* towards such an education, thus promising there could be some kind of educational technology that would work independently of the individuality of the learner or other situational conditions. As Comenius based his thoughts deeply in religious convictions, he may have had greater faith in the general similarities in human nature. Today, the notion of a supraindividual kind of education that would work for just anybody sounds a bit strange to us.

The term *didactics*, however, has been adopted widely since Comenius's days, but its increasing popularity came at the cost of it being expanded to cover a variety of different ideas, which may still be roughly categorised, however, as having an orientation towards technology on the one hand, or towards the well-being and development of the individual on the other. Against the background of contemporary achievements in learning theory, it is quite obvious that the traditional concept fails to address the complexity of the individual's learning processes. Yet this particular point of view is closely linked to the English usage of *didactics*.

The term 'didactics' has come to have a negative meaning in Anglo-American educational research and practice. Hamilton ... argues that this reflects definitions such as those given in the Oxford English Dictionary, that equate the term with 'formalist educational practices that combine "dogma" with "dullness"'. (Unwin, 2008, p. 509)

This, however, has not always been the case. When John Dewey described the term in the *Cyclopedia of Education* a hundred years ago, he still had a rather positive view of it (cf. Dewey, 1911; see also Friesen, 2007), even though the idea of using *one single* method still was apparent. In his short article, Dewey directly referred to the German tradition, in which didactics was an independent 'division of the many fields into which pedagogy in general is subdivided' (ibid.). Today, our understanding of didactics as the 'art and science of teaching' (ibid.), which aims at the individual's development and growth, is not restricted to the German use of the term but is also reflected in its use in other countries, including Scandinavia and many Eastern European countries. The French use of *didactics*, namely in the predominant concept of the *situation didactique* (Brousseau, 1998), also leads away from teacher-driven designs. Here, knowledge is considered to be

encapsulated in situations, and it is in going through those situations that the pupil, or whoever, can learn. This view of learning as 'learning form the situation' (much more than from the teacher, which is the institution's orthodox view of it) remains central to French didactics. (Chevallard, 2007, p. 132)

Keyword: Didactics

Following this 'continental' interpretation of the term, didactics in its different forms, can be described as systematic reflection about how to organise teaching in a way that brings about the individual growth of the student. This means that subject matters can open up different educative meanings for learners; and thus that teaching and learning follow different paths. (Hudson & Schneuwly, 2007, pp. 106–107)

To clarify which view on didactics they are referring to, some authors distinguish between the English *didactics* and the German *Didaktik*. Although this helps clarify the reference, it somehow obscures the Latin and Czech origins of the concept, its reception by people such as Dewey, and its meaning in other European areas. So even though we should remain well aware of the fact that *didactics* is sometimes understood in a rather limited way as a technology of learning, the wider meaning of the term shall serve as the basis for the discussions in this study guide.

However, to deal with the diverse meanings of didactics appropriately, we do have to introduce a German term, namely *Bildung*. The idea is of *Bildung* is closely related to the neo-humanist philosophy represented by Wilhelm von Humboldt (see also Chapters 3.2, 5.2). Although several volumes could be filled with contributions to a theory of *Bildung*, there are a few aspects that are particularly relevant for our further considerations here. *Bildung* is sometimes legitimately regarded as a somewhat blurred term. It is not easy to find an appropriate English translation (formation, education, and erudition are common candidates), but then again, the same is true of other philosophical terms that have been discussed mainly in one particular language area. Consequently, we follow the example of other authors and leave the word untranslated. *Bildung,* then, can be regarded as 'a state of being that can be characterised by a cluster of attributes described by terms such as "educated", "knowledgeable", "learned", "literary", "philosophical", "scholarly", and "wise"' (Hudson, 2007, p. 136).

Hudson describes the results of *Bildung,* and of course there are many other aspects to consider. Yet his description captures the idea of *Bildung* as a state of being rather than as a material possession. Furthermore, it is not a state of being that is reached at a certain age and then continues in a self-sustaining fashion; rather, it should be thought of as the result of ongoing strife. Like musical virtuosity or great athletic performance, *Bildung* is both: the result and the way to get there. For didactic considerations, this is of tremendous importance. Relating didactic action to *Bildung* the way it is done in the German discussion and elsewhere (cf. Biesta, 2009) means that learning outcomes are not to be evaluated by their usefulness for a particular domain of work or other practice, but always within a greater scheme of desirable outcomes of educational effort. The exact nature of these outcomes is a matter of the ongoing discussion on the theory of *Bildung*, but it is clear that any claim of supporting *Bildung* means supporting individual learners not only according to externally prescribed learning goals but also according to their individual needs as persons in the world.

7.2 Didactic models and models of instruction

No matter which term is used to describe formal teaching activity and the corresponding theoretical considerations, the area is obviously too promising not to invite the creation of certain concepts and models of teaching. Depending on their origin and focus, they may be called didactic models, designs, methodological concepts, or phase schemata. They all claim to provide a systematic and well-structured schema of actions and events that can be followed to achieve a specific learning result with a group of learners. Ideally, they are also supported by empirical evidence with respect to outcomes, as compared to other methodological approaches. Unfortunately, the latter requirement is the subject of constant debates about whether it is actually possible to evaluate the results of something as complex as a group of learners without accepting tremendous shortcomings in the validity of the results. This study guide is not the place to go into the details of this discussion, but we do have to make a few assumptions regarding this issue.

Obviously, learning research can be conducted in a way that delivers significant results concerning the relationship between a particular treatment ('method') and the results. The more researchers are able to keep those factors constant that are not in focus, the more precise their research will be. Accordingly, it is quite difficult to measure, let's say, the outcomes of two different treatments within a four-year programme in cultural studies. During the time of the course, students will be exposed to such a vast variety of influences that it will hardly be possible to determine which results can safely be attributed to the treatment. In principle, this objection holds for any learning research. Yet there are methodological as well as theoretical precautions that can be taken to reduce those risks. However, it seems impossible to obtain immediate results about the relationship between a treatment and its learning outcomes as long as there is no way of realising a laboratory-like research situation. If it is absolutely necessary to produce such results, they are likely to be produced by violating at least some of the methodological standards of quantitative research. Researchers and stakeholders who are forced to be accountable in such cases may find it difficult to act responsibly (cf. Pätzold, 2010c).

Empirical evidence for certain complex treatments (e.g. patterns of teaching methods) therefore often stems from research that covers only one part of the whole process. For example, researchers may measure learning outcomes in terms of what was remembered: they may focus only on a particular phase within the whole process, or they may incorporate research results from a different field that is regarded as analogous. Although this practice is both legitimate and necessary for investigating learning and teaching, it may contain pitfalls. The research could fail to record unexpected secondary effects, or the method of transferring findings from one field to another may be improper or flawed. All of these objections are not meant to question the relevance of empirical learning research in general, but to point out that any didactic approach is highly unlikely to generally prove superior to others. Rather, there will be evidence for the appropriateness of a certain treatment out of theoretical considerations (which themselves may indeed be tested empirically). For these reasons, concrete didactic models play a minor role in this study guide. Instead of giving an overview of the various models and the ways in which they are practised, criticised, and discussed, this chapter shall introduce three selected approaches *as examples* of didactic models. By that, it shall not be disputed that these models may be useful and important in both theory and practice. However, the models themselves cannot be regarded as 'learning theories'.

The first group of models is concerned with the temporal and systematic *sequence* of learning. In fact, one such model, Kolb's learning cycle, has already been mentioned (see Chapter 5). The idea of such *phase schemata* reaches back at least to the nineteenth century; in rudimentary form, phase schemata can be found in almost any formal teaching activity. A common and very basic example would be initiating the learning process by exposing learners to new content, then giving them the opportunity to experiment with it, then summarising important findings, and finally devoting time to practice.

Keyword: Phase schema

A phase schema provides a structured series of steps expected to occur during a learning process. It is used either as a model of learning (identifying the different steps of a more or less general sequence, that can be applied to various kinds of learning) or as a planning aid for teaching (suggesting certain steps regarded as useful to support learning).

Basically, phase schemata assume that learning takes place according to a sequence of distinct steps; hence teaching should provide the respective impulses and opportunities. If, for example, learning is regarded as the result of some experience of cognitive irritation that makes the learner look for information to resolve it, teaching could be organised by creating irritating experiences and then giving students hints on how to straighten things out again. It is generally accepted that, from a systematic point of view, such sequences do in fact exist (e.g. Piaget's process of equilibration), but it is difficult, if not impossible, to apply these to a general scheme. How much irritation is appropriate? When is the right time to provide hints to solve the issue? Which sequence of solutions is right if there are multiple reasons for irritation? Phase schemata have been discussed extensively in German didactics (cf. Jank & Meyer, 2009). They offer useful and sound suggestions for temporal and systematic structure as long as they are regarded as proposals rather than rigid and general templates for planning and conducting teaching. Besides, phase schemata are to be found in other approaches such as the following, known as cognitive apprenticeship.

Basically, this concept picks up ideas and structures from traditional craftsman apprenticeship training and transfers them to predominantly cognitive areas. Collins, Brown, and Newman (1989) introduced the term *cognitive apprenticeship* and applied it to domains such as writing and mathematics. The authors begin their argument by citing tradition, explaining that throughout history

apprenticeship was the most common means of learning and was used to transmit the knowledge required for expert practice in fields from painting and sculpting to medicine and law. Even today, many complex and important skills, such as those required for language use and social interaction, are learned informally through apprenticeship-like methods – that is, methods not involving didactic teaching, but observation, coaching, and successive approximation. (Collins et al., 1989, p. 1)

This quotation describes an approach to teaching that is surprisingly similar to that of Comenius. (And by the way, it also provides a good example of how the term *didactic* is used in a negative sense.). Like Collins et al., Comenius claimed that using teaching methods would help reduce the effort required by the teacher, and he devoted part of his studies to easing the learning of foreign languages (Comenius, 1657/1967, pp. 203ff.; Keatinge, 1967, p. 5). Ultimately, both approaches claim to promote a most 'natural' way of learning (cf. Collins et al., 1987, p. 28; Comenius, 1657/1967, e.g. pp. 127ff.).

According to cognitive apprenticeship, a teaching-learning sequence consists of six steps, which are usually called modelling, coaching, scaffolding (and fading), articulation, reflection, and finally, exploration (cf. Collins et al., 1989, pp. 16ff.). The sequence very much resembles that proposed by other phase models, but puts an emphasis on phases in which the learners are active. *Scaffolding*, for instance, means that students explore the applicability of newly acquired skills without having to completely master them in advance. The teacher, in this phase, merely provides some form of 'scaffolding' (ibid, p. 2) and step by step 'reduces his participation (fades), providing only limited hints, refinements, and feedback to the learner' (ibid., p. 3). The approach includes a number of further ideas, some of which are related to learning theory rather than to the apprenticeship model. For example, it emphasises that articulating one's knowledge is crucial for consolidating and developing it. The model of cognitive apprenticeship refers to the more general approach of situated learning (cf. Lave & Wenger, 1991), which originally referred to the observation of apprenticeship training in Western Africa (cf. Lave, 1977). In summary, cognitive apprenticeship stands for an eclectic approach based on history, contemporary observations of work life, and learning theory. Furthermore, it underscores the findings from reviews of existing empirical studies on learning and teaching, which are presented as 'success models for cognitive apprenticeship' (Collins et al., 1987, p. 5). The idea of cognitive apprenticeship has been quite influential, although this may partly be due to the fact that, to a certain extent, it relies on observations of good practice and its underlying concepts (a fact the authors do not deny). As a consequence, the concept as a whole today is more often discussed in textbooks on teaching than it is used in practice, where it rather serves as a collection of ideas for conducting lessons.

If cognitive apprenticeship stands for situational and eclectic concepts, the following approach by the German scholar Wolfgang Klafki stands for the attempt to create a didactic model that is all of one piece. The result has become known as *critical-constructive didactics*. Klafki's goal, from the beginning, was to link teachers' need to prepare for their lessons with a concept that was well founded in theory, rather independent of educational 'fashions', and still inspiring enough to foster creative didactic thought. He found the appropriate reference in *Bildung* (see above). As *Bildung* was regarded as the overall goal of all educational efforts, Klafki needed to clarify which learning matters actually contributed to it. To determine the value any such matter holds for achieving *Bildung*, Klafki formulated the following five basic questions:

- What is the matter's importance for the learner's presence?
- Equally, what is its importance for the learner's future?

- What does the matter stand for – that is, what does it exemplify with regard to which overall context?
- How can the learner actually access the matter – that is, what kind of prior knowledge and experience help facilitate learners' access to a new learning matter?
- How can learners show whether they were actually successful in learning the matter?

Klafki devoted much attention to the critical evaluation and justification of those questions on a philosophical basis. Thus his focus lay on the learning matter and the procedures for choosing it appropriately. Initially, Klafki was criticised for being not quite so careful in discussing the actual methods, however. After incorporating these critical comments in the further evolution of his model, Klafki eventually introduced the preliminary perspective chart (Figure 11). Here, the methodological structure has been included to take account of the fact that teaching methods and the learning matter are anything but independent of one another.

Figure 11: Klafki's preliminary perspective chart

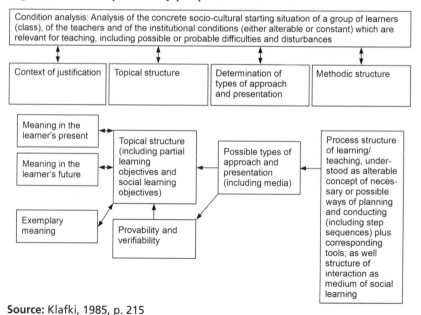

Source: Klafki, 1985, p. 215

Whereas the phase schema can be used to structure concrete lessons in a temporal and sequential way, the perspective chart provides a more systematic view of the issues to be considered when planning a lesson. It is well informed by theory, with the philosophy of education and *Bildung* playing a predominant role, but it can certainly not be called very practical. If phase schemata or cognitive apprenticeship are regarded as planning tools, then critical-constructive didactics is more of a means for reflection and justification. Still, all three perspectives contribute to the whole picture, as, for instance, critical-constructive didactics may more thoroughly inform our reflections on the person as a learner – a good deal of what belongs to a person is reflected in issues such as present meaning.

With this example, we shall conclude our overview of didactic models. As pointed out above, this study guide is not designed to provide concrete planning tools. Such tools are related to theories of education (and, sometimes, learning), but usually they are not theories in and of themselves. However, didactic models are sometimes considered indispensable as practical approaches for planning and reflecting on teaching activities. With that in mind, and with the help of some additional examples, we would like to encourage you to design your own didactic model, one firmly rooted in both theory and experience. To support you, the following sections shall elaborate on the aspects of learning that have already been carved out by our theoretical considerations in Part One, and link them to didactic conclusions.

Exercises and tasks

Exercise 1

Didactic models may serve as planning aids, but as rigid schemes of learning, they could also discourage creativity. Discuss the opportunities and risks provided by such models with respect to different situations in adult learning and teaching.

Exercise 2

Apply Klafki's perspective scheme to some teaching you have experienced. Where does it fit, where does it not fit? Can you think of stages in the teaching that could have been improved by considering Klafki's systematic ideas?

Task 1

Read an English-language document in which the German term *Bildung* is used as a loan word (e.g. Biesta, 2009, see below) and discuss whether referring to the German term is essential for the author's argument.

Biesta, G. (2009). *Educational research, democracy and TLRP*. Lecture presented at the TLRP event Methodological Development, Future Challenges, London, United Kingdom. Available at http://www.tlrp.org/dspace/handle/123456789/1620

Task 2

Read the 'Greeting to the reader' in Comenius's *Didactica Magna*. How would you translate this centuries-old mission of education to contemporary adult education? Which parts of it may be realistic, which parts may be utopian?

Comenius, J. A. (1657/1967). *Great didactic* (M. W. Keatinge, Trans.). New York: Russel & Russel.

8. Reflections on Learning

8.1 Learning and non-learning

Professionals in any field work to produce, maintain, or restore a certain state of affairs with respect to people, including the distribution of power or goods, personal situations, or the like. Lawyers and judges, for example, work to clarify legal relationships and administer justice; doctors strive to maintain or restore their patients' health; and librarians aim to provide customers with reading suggestions that match their interests. In each of these cases, there are basically two possibilities: either the professionals succeed in their effort or they fail. Obviously the same holds for members of the teaching profession: either they succeed in supporting learners with respect to learning impact, test results, and so forth, or they fail in the sense that learners do not achieve the desired learning outcomes. Yet their situation is a bit different from that in many other professions. As our discussion on learning up to his point has clearly shown, an individual learner's contribution to the learning process and its results is hardly to be overestimated. While there is no doubt that teachers and trainers can do a lot to facilitate learning, it is equally obvious that they are not at all capable of forcing somebody to learn once that person has, deliberately or not, decided not to learn. In contrast to what is often said, we cannot make somebody learn. All the teaching professional can do in that case is to create conditions to support the learning effort of the individual as much as possible. In some cases, this may even mean that the learner doesn't fully realise that he or she is actually learning. (Some types of 'edutainment' programmes obviously try to follow this path.) And yet, learning outcomes strictly depend on what happens on the learners' side. Learners' lived body and mind and their relationship to their material and social surroundings are crucial factors that can only be influenced or moderated by what a teacher, trainer, or facilitator does.

The term *prosumer* (originally coined by Alvin Toffler) is often used to describe a general shift in the production structures of Western societies, one in which the role of the consumer and that of the producer are partially merged. Originally, it was related to a variety of societal developments including the emergence of the do-it-yourself-sector, self-help in health care, and the use of media, but it can be applied to education as well (Arnold & Pätzold, 2008, p. 103). Learners may consume a certain service, such as a course or a lecture, to acquire a certain kind of skill, knowledge, or experience. Yet at the same time, they are producing these outcomes themselves, because the processing of what they undergo is bound to their own mental and bodily processes. Not only the satisfaction they may gain out of the experience but also the learning results themselves are learners' own products. More than three decades ago, Knowles made a strong point in his work on andragogy when he said that even though learners tended to rely on the support of teachers, experts, and advisers, as well as on media and tools, they still should be regarded as self-directed (cf. Knowles, 1975, p. 18). In other words, the learning results should be attributed to learners' own efforts. Or, as Jarvis put it, 'it is the person who learns' (Jarvis, 2006, p. 32).

We may still object that the situation is quite similar in the other professions mentioned above. A doctor, for example, may put a broken leg in splints, but it is the patient who, through his or her bodily functions, eventually helps close the fracture. Likewise, a librarian may suggest a most fascinating book or author, and yet the client might be displeased, possibly because of a bad mood or other circumstances that have nothing to do with the librarian's suggestion. These examples show that there are in fact a lot of situations in which a patient or customer may *influence* the actual use of a service, but the difference to learning is that there is absolutely no way to get around the learner's internal processes. A doctor may trust in the ability of bones to restore broken substance, but he may also use a prosthesis. An exciting book may fail to captivate a librarian's client, but on second thoughts, he or she would have to admit that it was unfavourable circumstances rather than a poor recommendation that kept him or her from enjoying the book.

Learning theory often underestimates or even completely ignores the interrelations between learner, teacher/trainer, and other learners, perhaps partly because of the complex nature of the relationship between provision and outcomes. Those branches of learning theory that define learning as a special type of mental process, therefore, have a particular tendency to deal only with the question of how learning occurs, whereas the question of what happens exactly when learning *does not* occur is often neglected. In recent literature, this issue has been addressed more frequently, however. For educational thinking, *non-learning* obviously is a serious issue. At the social level, it is addressed in terms of participation (at least as far as formal learning is concerned), whereas at the individual level, it may be considered as resulting from inappropriate teaching that doesn't match the needs of the learner. Moreover, non-learning may be related to the learner's physical condition (e.g. being tired, exhausted, etc.). But ultimately, it must also be considered as something emerging from the internal logic of the learner and therefore as something systematically hidden from complete outside observation.

In recent discussions, non-learning has not only begun to be regarded as a phenomenon worthy of investigation within learning research, but has also lost much of its one-sided, negative connotation. Jarvis, for example, included non-learning in his learning cycle as one of several possible results.

> **Keyword: Non-learning**
>
> A learner may go through a learning experience and come away as a changed person, but he or she may also emerge from the same experience more or less unchanged, as depicted in Jarvis' model of the learning cycle (see Figure 6).

Only if we define learning exclusively as a transformation of the person is non-learning an option not to be considered. But this stresses the point that learning results may differ considerably from teachers' intentions. In such cases, learners may have deliberately refused to comply with a certain learning task, but at the same time they may have learned something else (cf. Jarvis, 2009, p. 83). If we remember the perspective of Dewey, who saw learning as a fundamental developmental process within a democratic society, it becomes obvious that this type of learning is not just a possible secondary effect, but crucial for innovation. Refusing to learn what is taught officially and thereby learning something different has often turned out to be a driving force behind societal change. In this case, non-learning is the visible expression of learning resistance. To regard this occurrence of non-learning as deficient, or to assume that *nothing* at all has been learned, would be shortsighted (see also Faulstich & Grell, 2004).

At present, a single comprehensive theory of learning and non-learning does not exist. Although some authors (most notably Jarvis, Faulstich, Grell, and Illeris) address the issue of non-learning, their emphasis is still on the opposite process. Theories such as transformative learning do not deny the possibility of non-learning, but they put their focus differently. Scholars such as Klaus Holzkamp, a German psychologist who had a major influence on Illeris, on the other hand, tried to explain how and why non-learning may not only be a secondary effect but even the main result of certain kinds and circumstances of teaching (Holzkamp, 1995). For the following chapters on didactic issues, therefore, it is necessary to acknowledge that non-learning may occur at different levels, and that it does not necessarily indicate that either the facilitator or the learner have failed in their respective efforts. With that in mind, we may, as a starting point, look at one of your own learning experiences in the following exercise.

8.2 Exercise: Reflection on learning

This exercise is meant to present a number of practical results of our discussions of learning research up to this point. At the same time, it provides an opportunity for you to reflect upon your own learning by exploring a single learning process. The idea is to actualise your experience as a learner to form a basis for our discussion of the facilitator's perspective in the following sections. Below is a questionnaire I recently used in the context of learning research (cf. Pätzold, 2008). My aim was to apply findings from different learning theories to the self-reported learning experiences of adults. Although the focus is on learning in general, the questionnaire has also been used to differentiate learning processes according to different ages in order to identify the respective differences.

Like the participants in my research, you are now asked to fill in the questionnaire. Please select one of the learning tasks provided (or choose your own) and answer all the questions with respect to *this particular* learning process. For most of the questions, there are two scales: the first scale has five levels and asks for your level of agreement with the respective item; the second scale has only three levels and asks for your level of certainty regarding your answer. Most questions also provide an opportunity for taking notes. Completing the questionnaire may take about 20 minutes.

Figure 12: Questionnaire on an individual learning process

1a) Please select one item out of the following list of learning issues. All your answers in the following should refer to this item. If none of the suggestions appeals to you, please name one of your own and note it in the field 'other'.

1	Fractional arithmetic	
2	Classical music	
3	Lacing shoes	
4	Interest in politics/political awareness	
5	Bicycling	
6	Swimming	
7	Logical thinking	
8	Systems theory/constructivism	
9	Sports (which one?)	
10	Parlour game (which one?)	
11	Other	

1b) Please outline your learning issue. Did it concern basic knowledge or comprehensive ability; was it embedded in a broader learning project; etc.?

2) Please indicate when your learning process took place (please enter a year, a date, a school class, or something similar)

From	To	About this answer I am		
		sure O	partly sure O	unsure O
Notes				

83

3) Please rate the importance of other people during your learning process:

	Agreement (from ++: fully agree to --: fully disagree)					About this answer I am sure (+), partly sure (o), unsure (-)		
	++	+	o	-	--	+	o	-
Others were important as teachers.								
Others were important as partners in learning.								
Others were important because they were (independently) learning the same.								
Notes								

4) Learning doesn't only happen inside your head. Which role did your body play in your learning process?

	Agreement					sure (+) / unsure (-)		
	++	+	o	-	--	+	o	-
My body was important because the learning issue was a physical one.								
My body was important because the learning situation required physical efforts.								
There were physical requirements for entering the learning process.								
There were physical peculiarities (e.g. diseases) that influenced the learning process.								
The fact that my body changed during the learning process had an impact on my learning.								
Notes								

5) Aesthetics (beauty, taste, etc.) often play a role in learning. Please indicate the extent to which this was true in your case.

	Agreement					sure (+)/ unsure (-)		
	++	+	o	-	--	+	o	-
The learning issue itself had a certain aesthetic quality (beautiful, ugly, etc.).								
At least some of the learning media (books, board drawings) were excellently designed.								
In dealing with the learning issue, I acted in an aesthetic way (drawing pictures, moving, etc.).								
Learning the issue enabled me to do something else in an aesthetic way (e.g. using math to create graphs).								
Notes								

6) Did you learn the issue at least partly in a way that was different from school or similar modes:

	Agreement					sure (+) / unsure (-)		
	++	+	o	-	--	+	o	-
Learning mostly was embedded in my daily routines (work, hobbies, etc.).								
Learning mostly took place unconsciously.								
The individual learning occasions usually happened by coincidence.								
Learning mostly took place outside of a particular learning institution (school, adult education centres, etc.).								
I received considerable support from a teacher.								
Notes								

7) The following questions again address details of the learning process.

	Agreement					sure (+) / unsure (-)		
	++	+	o	-	--	+	o	-
Experience was important for the learning process.								
Routine was important for the learning process.								
I remember a lot of experiences I had during the learning process.								
During the learning process, I made a lot of mistakes.								
Making mistakes belongs to this learning process.								
In case I made mistakes during the learning process, it did not have serious negative consequences.								
Due to the learning process, I forgot other things.								
Due to the learning process, other things I knew or could do before lost their validity.								
Acquiring knowledge played an important role during the learning process.								
Acquiring skills played an important role during the learning process.								

Notes

8) The following questions address further conditions of the learning process.

	Agreement					sure (+)/ unsure (-)		
	++	+	o	-	--	+	o	-
I dealt with the learning issue on a voluntary basis.								
yIn dealing with the issue, I continued learning in an area in which I learned before (but was interrupted).								
The fact that I dealt with this learning issue at precisely this moment was coincidental.								
In retrospect, the learning process has benefitted my occupational development.								
In retrospect, the learning process has benefitted my personal development.								
At the beginning of the learning process, the issue was highly important to me ('presence importance').								

	++	+	o	-	--	+	o	-
At the beginning of the learning process, I expected the issue to become important to me in the future ('future importance').								
At present, it is quite useful for me to have gone through the learning process.								
At the beginning of the learning process, I was about...	...years old.							

Notes

11) Finally, a few questions regarding your personal impressions of the learning process.

	Agreement					sure (+)/ unsure (-)		
	++	+	o	-	--	+	o	-
The learning process affected me emotionally.								
The skills I acquired in the learning process have changed me as a person.								
The knowledge I acquired in the learning process has changed me as a person.								
Due to the learning process, my relationship to others has changed.								
Due to the learning process, my outlook on the world has changed.								
Overall, I experienced the learning process as difficult.								
Back then, I was very motivated to engage in the learning process.								
Back then, I was interested in the learning issue.								
I would have missed out on a lot if I hadn't dealt with the learning issue.								

Notes

Source: own source

As mentioned above, the questionnaire originally served as a research instrument. It was completed by about 200 people of different ages, who referred to a wide variety of learning issues. After completing the questionnaire yourself, you may be interested in some of the results. First of all, the answers proved that the general ideas of a pedagogical learning theory, as discussed in this text, can in principle be covered by questionnaires like the one above. The aspects of time, person, and lifeworld (mentioned in the introduction and in Chapter 5.1) could, to a certain extent, be represented in the questionnaire, and it has been shown that there is a corresponding variety of significantly different ratings of the various items and item clusters. With respect to the person as a learner, for example, it could be shown via factor analysis that aspects of motivation on the one hand and of emotion on the other could quite precisely be distinguished from other person-related variables. With respect to age, it could be shown for a variety of variables that, sometimes contrary to my theoretical assumptions, outcomes did in fact not vary significantly between different age groups.

To examine the impact of age, the data were divided into two groups: one group reporting learning processes that took place before the age of 18 and one reporting more recent processes. It turned out that the results were the same in both groups regarding, for example, the body as a matter of learning, the extent to which the learning process contributed to personal development, and the importance of the learning matter. Significant differences, in contrast, emerged with respect to learning circumstances. As expected, the learning of adults was more often reported as voluntarily and as building on some prior learning. These findings changed partially when the dividing age was lowered from 18 to nine years. At this age, physical development is at the foreground of our experience, and so are the respective (learning) activities. Differences therefore were more pronounced here, but mainly with regard to physical aspects that were much more in focus as learning matters in this group than in the learning processes taking place after the age of nine. In summary, the comparison of adult and younger learners has shown that general variables of a learning process – that is, those related to learning as a change of the person in the world – do not differ between adult learners and adolescents and children, if the age of 18 is used to separate the two groups. Differences in the learning processes of younger and older learners may occur if there are (age-related) differences concerning the learning matter and if those (age-related) differences in turn influence the differences in question. This is particularly true of learning in which the body is important as a learning matter, as these types of learning processes are much more frequently experienced by children than by adults.

Now let's return to the issue of teaching. The goal of the above exercise was to raise our awareness of the various aspects of the learning process as discussed in previous chapters: time or change, person, and lifeworld. In the following chapters, we are going to address these aspects mainly from a didactic perspective. While doing so, we have to keep in mind that they originally stem from theories about learning. When, for example, the phenomenographers (see Chapter 3.1) state that learning becomes evident in a changed relationship between the person and the object, they do not necessarily claim that teaching or facilitating has to aim at producing this change directly. One way of teaching could be to ask the learner to express his or her view of an object and then to construct a case in which this view may turn out useless. Another way could be to provide a more elaborate view and leave it to the learner to compare the two. A third way could be to deal with the various views within a group, either theoretically or empirically through experiments. All of these ways may be appropriate, but neither of them directly aims at triggering a particular change in a certain direction. So again we have to recall the facilitative nature of teaching and the fact that teaching, due to the inescapable internal logic of the individual, can only be an attempt. A review of the learning process you dealt with in the questionnaire might underpin those issues, especially if you recall the role of others in your learning. With that in mind, we shall now, in the following chapters, explore the three cornerstones time, person, and lifeworld from a didactical point of view.

Exercises and tasks

Exercise 1

Compare your questionnaire results with those of other students. Are there unexpected differences or general tendencies?

Task 1

In my research, I related some of the results from the questionnaire to participants' educational biographies (see Pätzold, 2011). Which links do you see between your results and your own previous educational experience and practice? Compare your conclusions to those reported in the article.

Pätzold, H. (2011). Emotions, the person and the 'lived body': Learning experiences and impacts from the 'pedagogical orientation'. ROSE: *Research on Steiner Education, 2(1)*. Available at www.rosejourn.com

9. Time, Person, Lifeworld: Cornerstones of Didactic Theory

9.1 Time: Sequences and gestalt of learning

Learning requires time. If you completed the questionnaire in the previous chapter, you also indicated the time it took you to master the learning issue (Question 2). It may have been a very short period of time (e.g. to learn the basics of a game), or it may have taken years (e.g. to master a musical instrument). In both cases, a few or many other activities usually took place simultaneously. Learning a musical instrument does not fully occupy one's time, and learning to play a parlour game, which usually serves entertainment purposes, typically involves a lot of chit-chat and fun. Yet even learning a single name or a phone number requires a certain amount of time during which we are unable to pay full attention to other things. There is no doubt that cognitive processes, even though they sometimes seem to happen very quickly, do need time. Nervous impulses have to go through neurons, be passed on from one to another, and be processed in various ways.

Any cognitive effort may serve as an example. Picture your own face in your mind, for example, and focus on the area around your left eye. Although there is no mechanical process involved, it may have taken you some time, first, to create an image of yourself, and then to concentrate on a particular area within that image. Regardless of whether you were successful or not, this little exercise should have given you an idea of the time consumed by mere thinking. Obviously, the same conditions apply to learning, or at least to the cognitive part in learning. But the amount of time consumed by learning is not limited to the runtime of nerve impulses. All of us are quite familiar with learning tasks that require not only regular 'processing time', but also interruptions during which our attention is directed towards other things. For example, a long distance runner could not condense his weekly training to a single 24-hour session. Similarly, it is impossible to condense the preparations for a difficult exam to a single multiple-hour session (though we may sometimes be tempted to try). Obviously, breaks are sometimes needed, and there is strong evidence suggesting that those breaks do not just serve relaxation purposes but are partly filled with unconscious nerve activity and restructuring that fosters the learning process unnoticeably.

Furthermore, learning processes may differ vastly depending on the time that is available for learning. Although most people would surely be able to recognise a sunflower when they see one, the majority of them probably wouldn't be able to tell whether its leaves grow alternately or in pairs. As long as they are not particularly interested in botany, most people would rather have set up a conception of the gestalt of a sunflower than of its specific systematic characteristics (in the same way we are usually able to recognise familiar people without always being able to name specific visual features such as a beard, glasses, etc.). This type of learning usually does not require much effort but may take quite long. If, by contrast, we would have to learn to recognise and differentiate a certain number of plants in a short period of time, we would probably not attempt to learn them the same way, but would try to remember the characteristics we consider to be relevant and easy to remember, even though they may not necessarily contribute to the overall appearance of the plant. In Jarvis's learning cycle (see Figure 6), this would mean going straight from the situation to memorising without taking any unnecessary detours that might lead to further experience, reflection, and the like.

With this example, two rather broad-brush sketches of how learning processes may look like have emerged: a holistic or gestalt-oriented, non-systematic, time-consuming, and easy way on the one hand, and a detail-oriented, systematic, quick, and often arduous one on the other. Of course, they can only be distinguished analytically, because in reality, they will often be mixed. Their relation to time is not limited to their own duration, however, but also includes the learner's biography. Toddlers, for example, learn about the world not by fitting things into a system but by developing systems out of what they learn and experience. Piaget has shown crucial steps in this process, such as the evolution of a child's concept of numbers. The more formal learning becomes, the more it gravitates towards the other side of the induction/deduction dichotomy. Systems become more important, and the holistic experience is left for less formalised areas. Certain methods of teaching, however, try to reconnect learning to the holistic approach by preferring experience over systems – that is, by leaving the construction of systems more to the individual. From a constructivist point of view, this preference seems justified, but there are equally strong arguments against it. Phenomenography, for example, thinks of learning as a change in the relationship between the learner and the object, so a *system* of whatever origin can only serve as a *mediator* for this relationship and its alteration. Thus it may be useful to initiate the systematic learning process while knowing that the system itself would not count as the final objective.

> **Keyword: Self-directed learning**
>
> The concept of self-directed learning and its derivatives represent some of the didactic conclusions drawn from these thoughts about learning. Self-direction in learning gives learners the opportunity to adjust their learning path to their individual needs and desires. Particularly, it allows learners to individually allocate their available time to different learning tasks.

There are many approaches that seek to introduce this concept to formal education. Some of the most popular ones are related to the educational approach of Maria Montessori. A quite prominent concept used here (and in other educational approaches as well) is the weekly plan. The core idea of this approach, which was originally designed for school teaching and elementary education, is to assist students with setting up an individual plan containing the tasks to be completed within one week. A weekly plan helps learners structure their time and effort and encourages them to develop a realistic view of the relationship between their tasks and the time available. Moreover, it serves as an informal evaluation tool to document and review what has been achieved at any given point. In adult education seminars, it is quite common for teachers and participants to set up a schedule for the whole seminar together. Often this is done in a brainstorming session and with the help of cards containing certain objectives to be achieved. These cards are then attached to a notice board to be sorted and evaluated. This method may foster the feeling of engaging in a shared effort, but it does not address the needs of individual learners because they are expected to contribute – and possibly subordinate – their own expectations to a joint decision. Approaches of learning advice are a bit closer to the work plan idea because their aim is to concretely assist the learner with setting up an individual plan. Putting this into the framework of a formal weekly work plan, as Montessori pedagogy does, connects the core idea of self-direction with the social side of formal learning efforts.

The corresponding didactic considerations are underpinned by learning theories in many ways. The general idea of self-direction has already been mentioned. The social aspect refers to Illeris's learning triangle, among other concepts. Here the importance of being an individual learner in a social context is emphasised. From this point of view, it is important that planning (such as making a weekly work plan or something similar) is, on the one hand, an individual activity (as a single plan will not suit all learners), but on the other is done on the basis of a general agreement. The latter aspect helps ensure that there are regular opportunities to present, discuss, or evaluate results. According to Illeris and Jarvis, however, this ongoing review is rather a means than an end. As learning is an effort undertaken in a social surrounding, it should be important to know and feel that others are undertaking the same effort. This hypothesis is supported by the research mentioned above. In the questionnaire presented in Chapter 8.2, 46 per cent of respondents agreed or fully agreed with the statement that other people were important for their learning because they were (independently) learning the same.

From the perspective of self-directed learning, teaching may, to a large extent, be devoted to organising frameworks of time during which learning may take place. And a look beyond the realm of organised education soon reveals that the history of educational institutions in society can be read as a history of making time available for individuals to learn. Historically, enforcing compulsory school attendance first and foremost meant releasing children from performing other duties. Today, struggles between labour unions and employers are often about the question of how much of their working time employees may use for further education. Recent developments in higher education take this into account: reformers have made great efforts to define students' workload as a measure for the estimated time required for learning something. The German didactic tradition in particular features a variety of attempts to construct appropriate time schemes. Although they sometimes tended to be quite rigid (and did not always adequately address the challenge of diversity in learning groups), they still highlighted the fact that learning does not only require phases of instruction and explanation but also structured and valued time to think about, discuss, and experiment with the content.

Thoughts about the time structure within the process of learning generated ideas about a gestalt of learning, which brings us back to the process models of learning. Kolb's learning cycle served as an example of how learning, in analytical terms, proceeds from one step to the next; obviously, this can also be thought of as a progression in time. Yet the two dimensions must not be mixed arbitrarily, as it is often difficult to actually observe the temporal sequence of steps that are easily identified from an analytical standpoint. Bateson used the term *punctuations* to address this issue (Bateson, 1972, p. 162), stating that processes of learning, like other processes, could be subdivided into many different ways depending on the observer's point of view. Ultimately, it is the learner who has to take charge of his or her learning process, especially if learning is situated in an environment based on concepts of self-directed learning. In such instances, self-observation, including the choice of appropriate punctuations, is a crucial task for the individual. In this respect, teaching includes counselling learners and supporting them in developing the ability to plan and review their learning, especially with respect to the required amount of time.

9.2   Person: Emotion, cognition, and the lived body

The German Institute of Adult Education (DIE) recently held a conference on learning and movement (see also DIE, 2011). 'Movement' in this case was not primarily meant metaphorically (even though the history of adult education is full of movement-related metaphors), but literally: the main part of the conference was devoted to the relationship between adult learning and the movement of the body. Conferences such as this one can be seen as indicators of a growing awareness of the body as an influential and inescapable factor of learning. Just as the importance of emotions for adult education was widely rediscovered in the 1990s, it now seems the discussion has turned to the body. However, emotions and cognition also have to be integrated in any concept of learning that claims to cover the whole person. The theoretical approaches discussed in Part One have provided a few insights in this context.

Emotional aspects of learning have been discussed in most of the contemporary contributions to learning theory, particularly in those by Illeris, Jarvis, and Gieseke. Illeris regards learning as a process involving a kind of balance between cognition and emotion. Whereas cognition is predominantly responsible for the actual acquisition of the learning matter, emotions accompany the process – but in a way, they also provide (or withhold) the required energy (see Chapter 2.2). From our everyday experience, this is quite obvious. If we have a positive attitude towards a learning matter, we find it easy to spend our time exploring it, and we are more likely to engage even in boring tasks such as learning vocabulary if they are associated with positive feelings. Furthermore, it has been shown that negative emotions such as anxiety tend to inhibit learning (at least learning the matter that is being taught, cf. Niemi, 2009, pp. 3–4; Gieseke, 2007, pp. 65ff.). In this case, theories of biological origin on the one hand and approaches such as humanist psychology on the other lead to similar results. In a state of anxiety, we are not likely to be open to new learning opportunities; we rather tend to search for a way out of the intimidating situation. Actually, this tendency has probably proved useful throughout the phylogenetic development of humans: facing an imminent danger, our ancestors were well advised to concentrate on utilising their abilities to avoid or defend against it (e.g. by hiding, fighting, deceiving, or running from the cause of danger). *Later* there would be time to reflect on the situation and maybe learn from it. Humanist psychologists would argue that there is no need for nourishing a desire for learning on the part of the subject because the urge for development and growth is given inherently. Therefore, an individual's non-engagement in a given situation is not a reason for punishment but for adjusting the situation to the individual's needs and conditions.

These thoughts suggest that we should try to avoid the occurrence of negative emotions in teaching situations, but the wider question about the general role of emotions in learning remains to be addressed. Emotions have been regarded as a source of energy, yet this proposition, too, has to be examined further. Jarvis suggested that learning generally occurs in situations of 'disjuncture' (Jarvis, 2009, p. 20) – that is, each time a general feeling of harmony between our knowledge and our experience of the world is interrupted. This idea resembles Festinger's theory of cognitive dissonance or Piaget's strive for equilibration, for example. What is unique to Jarvis's idea of 'disjuncture' is that he sees the feeling of harmony from an emotional point of view and, again, that it is the whole person who strives to reinforce this feeling. In other words, it is this feeling that drives or motivates us to undertake any effort related to learning, whether it be physical (e.g. going to find a learning resource), cognitive (e.g. concentrating on a tricky problem), or emotional (e.g. continuing to study instead of engaging in more comfortable occupations). From a didactic perspective, the obvious consequence would be to arrange learning situations in which learners may experience disjuncture without feeling so unsettled as to be uncomfortable.

Yet emotions play a further role in learning insofar as they determine the relationship between the various actors involved. In Chapter 6.2, we already mentioned the mirror neurons as a means of understanding other people's mental states. In other words, these mirror neurons enable us to 'attune' ourselves to others' emotions and thereby to share others' feelings in a certain situation. Gieseke states that 'emotions form the bridge to the other, which makes communication possible' (Gieseke, 2007, p. 15). The learner as a person thus is *emotionally embedded* in a learning situation, and hence dependent on other subjects. From a didactic point of view, this means that emotions are not just something learners may be permitted to show in learning situations, but rather something to be welcomed to a certain extent, because only through emotions may a number of disconnected learners build a learning group. Any concept of social learning, from simple group work to learning communities, would therefore require learners to form some kind of emotional tie between each other. But even though having emotions (and actually *expressing* them) is necessary, emotions also need to be controlled.

The importance of controlling or 'managing' emotions, as some people would put it, is not only a concern in pedagogy but in theories of modernisation generally (cf. van der Loo & van Rejen, 1992). According to Jarvis, who deals with the issue briefly (cf. Jarvis, 2009, pp. 143–144), it is an important learning goal, because controlling our emotions (and more specifically, controlling the ways we *show* our emotions) has to be seen as an important key competence for social and economic participation. However, managing emotions is already a key part of the *individual's* learning efforts. As pointed out above, emotions act as a kind of gatekeeper that either fosters or inhibits our engagement in learning activities. If a learning matter seems to be of no interest, we are rather unlikely to pay attention to it without external pressure or other internal sources of motivation. In either case it would be useful to create or at least discover positive emotions towards the learning matter. One way could be, for example, to explore whether something interesting might yet be found in the learning matter; another would be to imagine positive experiences with its application in a different context. Strategies like these are called 'metacognitive' (Niemi, 2009, p. 3) because they go beyond a certain cognitive process. Although the term suggests that metacognition is mainly a cognitive process, it needs to be emphasised that the process is closely linked to the emotional side as well. Cognitive tasks (such as learning vocabulary) require the subject to decide in favour of the task (and against alternatives). This will positively not happen simply because of rational arguments. Rather, it requires the *person* to be in an emotional state that allows him or her to devote cognitive effort to a given task.

Sometimes emotional obstacles to learning are obvious (e.g. feeling scared or threatened), but, as Illeris's model has shown, any kind of learning is accompanied by emotions that are, in some way or another, suitable for keeping up the learning process. These emotions do not have to be closely linked to the learning matter itself – I might be bored by math, for example, while feeling positive about myself as a diligent student no matter what the topic – though it would often be desirable. Metacognition regularly seeks to support this, and a lot of course methods do so as well. One example would be the 'advance organiser' (Ausubel, 1960). Ausubel argued that to foster learning and the retention of new knowledge it was helpful to establish a link with learners' existing knowledge. Although he was arguing strictly from a cognitivist point of view, the general idea also works with the person-related perspective and the corresponding thoughts on emotions. Being able to link new matter to our existing knowledge strengthens the feeling that it is indeed a relevant part of our lifeworld and that, despite its being new, we are generally able to master it based on our existing abilities. As a result, we are less likely to feel disoriented or even threatened.

Up until now, our perspective on emotions has mainly been analytical. As we have seen, emotions are an integral part of any learning because they belong to the person and are necessary for providing the kind of 'energy' or 'drive' that will help that person make the cognitive (and physical) effort to address the learning task at hand. Emotions, however, may also be seen as a bodily phenomenon in and of themselves. This proposition is not meant to argue in favour of a mere materialistic reductionism, but there can be no doubt that emotions are, at least to a certain extent, related to bodily processes. Emotions may occur along with neuronal activity, the release of hormones, a change in blood pressure, and so forth. But saying that 'emotions occur along with ...' means dividing the process into two distinct aspects: on the one hand, there are emotions; on the other hand, there are bodily processes to accompany them. Philosophically, this is an instance of the body-mind problem that goes back to Descartes and has been widely discussed both in pragmatism and the philosophy of mind (cf. Ryle, 1990). The question whether these two are separate processes (a Cartesian view), whether emotions are merely a secondary effect of bodily processes (a materialistic perspective), or whether both represent different categories of thinking (Ryle's approach) is serious enough to be mentioned here, but – fortunately from an educational perspective – the consequences are largely similar. The phenomenon of emotions, to say the least, must be regarded as something that simultaneously affects body *and* mind.

It was predominantly the area of workplace learning in which the importance of the body was recognised. Workplace learning often involves psychomotor learning goals; from there, one does not have to go far to see the body's pervasive influence on learning in general. Researchers in this area adopted an 'embodied view' (Hodkinson, Biesta, & James, 2008, p. 31) of learning. The diversity of approaches towards the relationship of mind and body notwithstanding, educational researchers who deal with the issue at all tend to adopt a phenomenological perspective. In this line of thinking, the traditional term is the German word *Leib,* or 'lived body'.

> **Keyword: Lived body/*Leib***
>
> The phenomenological term *Leib*, usually translated as 'lived body', re-
> fers to the surplus beyond the consideration of the mere physical body.
> Whereas the body may be regarded as as a separate entity (the sen-
> tence 'my leg is aching' means that it is me who experiences the pain;
> however, it also means that 'my leg' is something separate from me),
> the *Leib* is inseparable from the individual human. 'From the body, our
> I is different. We live with the body. With our *Leib*, we are one.' (Bas-
> feld, 2008, p. 208, own translation)

According to phenomenology, the importance of the lived body goes far beyond emotions on the one hand and movement on the other. In fact, the body plays a role in each single instance of perception. What we perceive in the first place is influenced by our position in space. For instance, when watching a bird fly across a cloudless sky, it is the movement of our eyes or head that actually give us the impression that the bird is in fact moving. Moreover, the body is a kind of geometrical 'zero-point' (Thompson & Zahavi, 2007, p. 80) towards which we relate our spatial experience of any object in the surrounding area. The person-centred perspective implies regarding the body as crucial for learning simply because it is an integral part of the person. Furthermore, social interaction – an important part of learning – deeply depends on bodily aspects as well: think of the body's contribution to communication, for example. Ultimately, we may wonder whether any and all learning processes can be regarded as being influenced by the body. Returning, once again, to the questionnaire in Chapter 8.2, you might refer to your own case and consider the extent to which bodily aspects seemed important in your learning process. Of course, the answer will largely depend on the specific learning issue. Learning how to calculate with fractions will be regarded as less body-related than learning how to swim, for example. Yet the corresponding empirical data show that even in cases in which the learning issue does not seem to have any immediate bodily relevance, respondents rarely answered that the body had no significance at all (cf. Pätzold, 2008).

The didactic conclusions drawn from these findings are manifold. Involving the body (e.g. through movement) may serve to support the learning process. With respect to the learning matter, bodily experiences can help learners perceive the matter as something that is not exclusively related to cognition. Students many not only assume a certain position in a classroom discussion by stressing a particular point, but also literally by moving to a certain place inside the classroom. As a result, the distribution of opinions within a group and the effort involved in changing one's position can be experienced holistically, which may lead to discussions about the similarities between adopting a position mentally and spatially. Many action-oriented methods in adult education are suitable for exploring and fostering bodily involvement in learning. Yet these methods are bound to be underestimated as long as they are only regarded as stimulating alternatives to traditional teaching methods. As such, they may be used to great benefit, but their full potential lies in involving the whole person in a subject-related learning experience. Ultimately, learning through the body, or 'embodiment' (Freiler, 2008, p. 40), can be seen as 'a way to construct knowledge through direct engagement in bodily experiences and inhabiting one's body through a felt sense of being-in-the-world' (ibid.).

The fact that emotions and the lived body have gradually received the recognition they deserve within the interplay of the various aspects of the whole person can be regarded as a sign of significant progress in the recent history of the social sciences in general and of pedagogy in particular. Experimental neuroscience has even shown that some mental processes that were traditionally regarded as rational decisions must rather be seen as emotional ones, which only afterwards are amended by rational arguments. These experiments, introduced by Libet (1978), reveal the complex nature of the relationship between emotion and cognition, but to cite them as evidence of a general predominance of emotions is to overestimate their results (cf. Meyer-Drawe, 2008, p. 129). Generally, it seems that some authors try to wage a kind of battle in which emotions (or emotions and the body) are pitted against cognition. In fact, we do not have sufficient knowledge to make final judgements on issues like this; at the same time, there can be no doubt that processes such as learning simultaneously involve both sides. It is a welcome development, therefore, that the formerly underestimated aspects of emotions and the lived body are now increasingly taken into account, and yet it must by no means result in an underestimation of the cognitive aspect of learning. Each of the theoretical approaches presented in Part One therefore addresses the cognitive side, albeit to a different degree. Illeris, for example, puts emotions and cognition alongside each other (while rather neglecting the body, as we have seen), thus emphasising their equal importance in learning. Jarvis's comprehensive theory of learning doesn't focus on any of the three aspects specifically – most of the steps in his learning cycle can be discussed from an emotional, a bodily, or a cognitive perspective. Nevertheless, his definition of learning (see Chapter 5.1) explicitly covers all three dimensions.

From among the more recent concepts, the phenomenographic approach can be regarded as the 'most cognitive' one. Although Marton and his colleagues do certainly not conceptualise learning as a process devoid of emotional influence, the strength of their idea of progress in learning through a change in the way someone sees something rather lies in modelling the cognitive side. Experiencing a phenomenon thus can be seen as a process in which individuals *interpret* their experience against an internal concept. Up to this point, phenomenography, cognitive psychology, and constructivism describe the process in similar terms. Learning then may occur if the individual, for whatever reason, fails to find an interpretation that matches the internal concept. One reaction, of course, might be to avoid the experience altogether. (Here, the connection between learning and emotions in general and the concept of non-learning in particular emerge.) Yet the phenomenographers care more about the transition from one internal concept to the next. Their core idea is that the irritation caused by the lack of an appropriate interpretation leads to a change in the internal concept.

Now this is the point at which phenomenography, cognitive psychology, and constructivism part ways. Basically, cognitivism assumes the internal concept to improve continuously until it becomes more and more like reality itself. Internal concepts, in other words, tend to create an image of the outside world. Constructivism, by contrast, essentially considers those internal concepts to be entirely idiosyncratic. Therefore they can neither be regarded nor tested as reflections of an external reality. As a result, there are as many internal concepts as there are individuals, and comparing them directly is virtually impossible. The phenomenographers adopt a rather persuasive intermediate position. Although they acknowledge that accessing a person's internal concepts is indeed impossible, their research approach still enables them to show the outlines of these concepts. Furthermore, phenomenographic research underpins the hypothesis that, even though the details of any internal concept may vary from one person to another, there are general similarities between those concepts, and they can often be ordered in a progressive way. As we have seen in our earlier example, the concept of a thermostat as a valve can clearly be distinguished from that of a thermostat as a control circuit, regardless of the possible variance *within* those two concepts. Finally, those different views do not refer to a given, absolute reality, but to the lifeworld of the individual. 'Learning is seen as a change in the learner's capability of experiencing a phenomenon in the world around them' (Marton & Pang, 1999, p. 9), which again depends on the individual's view of it. An obvious consequence is that a person may fail to understand a certain concept not because of a lack of cognitive abilities (although that could be an additional explanation) but primarily because what is to be understood does not match the needs and requirements of that person's lifeworld.

The phenomenographic approach has been designed to explain aspects of learning with respect to real-world situations in schools and other educational institutions. This is why there are lots of didactic conclusions and recommendations, which range from detailed advice on how to teach certain subjects to very general ideas. It is impossible to present and discuss all of them in depth here. Instead, the following paragraphs will concentrate on some of the typical and rather general consequences, thereby relating them to other aspects of this study guide.

The phenomenographic approach emphasises variation. Since internal concepts become clearer when they are contrasted with alternative concepts, there must be a source for variety in our experience and interpretation of phenomena. Phenomenographic research has shown that those variations should be manifold. One traditional and quite well-known approach is to teach a grammar rule, for example, by applying it to a variety of different sentences. However, from a phenomenographic perspective, this would not be enough variation because the rule to be used is always the same. On the contrary, there should not only be a variety of different applications but also a variety of different grammar rules to be applied at the same time. This is unproblematic from a systematic point of view, but it leads back to the issue of emotions. It has proven useful to experience the abovementioned type of difference in a learning situation, because one 'crucial aspect of learning is the ability of discerning differences and variation' (Melander, 2009, p. 121). Yet it will at the same time be irritating and maybe even threatening because those variations inevitably come along with a certain lack of orientation, which could cause a feeling of discomfort. The variations provided and experienced may nourish the cognitive process of learning, but at the same time emotional obstacles may occur if the level of irritation is not well balanced with respect to the learner.

When phenomenography was first developed, one major question to be answered was, 'Why do students learn different things from identical texts?' This observation may apparently be explained by a variety of factors including prior knowledge, time available, general reading skills, and so on, but systematic differences between students still seemed to remain, which Marton and his colleagues hypothetically assumed to be differences in the very process of learning. Some students investigated the text, raised questions they tried to answer, and generally sought to arrive at a full understanding; as a result, they were able to discuss, criticise, or apply its contents. Other students rather tried to figure out only the most important bits of information and prepared to reproduce them when questioned; of course, there were many positions in between. The two ends of this learning continuum are usually called *deep approach* versus *surface approach* (or sometimes 'strategic learning', Coffield, Moseley, Hall, & Ecclestone, 2004, p. 65).

> **Keywords: Deep approach versus surface approach**
>
> A surface approach to learning basically refers to learning that is aimed at merely reproducing material in a test or exam (e.g. by rote memorisation of certain terms without considering their interrelations). Following a deep approach, in contrast, means engaging seriously with an issue, guided by a desire for understanding rather than by the need to comply with external demands.

Those differences in students' learning processes in fact lead to different learning outcomes, which range from mere knowledge of some of the given facts (with few or even no ideas regarding their relationship) to a concise understanding of the presented issue and knowledge of the facts, too (cf. Marton & Säljö, 2005). If deep understanding is desired, one obvious didactic consequence would be to instruct students to apply the deep approach from the very beginning. However, the experiment conducted to test this strategy produced different results: compared to the control group, the students who were instructed to apply the deep approach turned out to be less successful. Marton and Säljö argued that this was 'a special case of the common human experience of transformation of means into ends' (ibid., p. 51). It should also be kept in mind that the students in the experiment, in contrast to those applying the deep approach spontaneously, did not raise their *own* questions about the text. Whereas spontaneous questions focus on irritations or mismatches between the reading experience and students' internal concepts, questions prescribed by the instructor simply come across as tasks or exercises. The didactic conclusions, therefore, must go a bit deeper.

Modelling a deep approach by suggesting supportive activities (e.g. 'write down the most important concepts', 'answer the following questions', 'create a diagram showing the relationship between the two theories', etc.) probably won't escape all the shortcomings of the surface approach. In fact, it may even lead to lower levels of achievement. This may be avoided, however, by considering the emotional side as well, and by clearly offering tasks as suggestions rather than compulsory exercises. But if facilitators or teachers want their students to apply the deep approach to a learning matter, they cannot help presenting and situating the matter in a way in which it is appropriate for their students to spontaneously handle it according to the deep approach – 'if we want to promote a deep approach, we should above all keep in mind the students' own interest at the same time as we should try to eliminate the factors that lead to a surface approach (irrelevance, threat and anxiety)' (Marton & Säljö, 2005, p. 54). Obviously this is no easy task, and above all, it shows the inevitable experimental side of education and teaching, as too much of the learning process – emotionally, bodily, and cognitively – occurs on the student's side and can only be influenced indirectly by others, if at all. Nevertheless, offering connections to learners' interests, respecting their emotions (positive or negative) regarding a certain matter, and creating opportunities to experience both the appropriateness and the shortcomings of one's own concept of that matter may serve as a profound basis for making learners more likely to use the deep approach.

The phenomenographic approach has inspired a wide range of research on very different subjects. Among the topics that have received the most constant attention has been the evolution of the concept of learning itself. Here, the question has been how students think about the issue and learning, and which factors may serve to change their perspective. The core idea is that certain subjects and certain learning situations require a particular attitude towards learning, along with the respective abilities and skills. With respect to university courses, for example, Smith and Blake (2009) stated:

As learners and their teachers are exposed to the different sectors there is a need to develop cross-sectoral understanding of what learning can mean if we are to avoid confusion in expected learning outcomes and learning experiences. (p. 234)

Marton and his colleagues developed a hierarchy of learning approaches, discussed earlier in this book (see Chapter 3.1). To find out about such concepts is important for general learning research, but it may also have an impact on learners themselves. The difference between the surface and deep approaches is one instance of this impact. It goes without saying that the deep approach will generally result in much more sustainable learning outcomes. It would be short-sighted, however, not to consider the impact of different learning concepts in the opposite direction as well (cf. Coffield et al., 2004, p. 25). As learning is a time-consuming process (see Chapter 9), the question is not only how to improve the results in terms of retention, for example, but also to support learners in managing their (temporal) resources efficiently. According to the learning stages described by phenomenography, 'understanding' would be the minimum stage that should be achieved by someone dealing with an introduction into a subject he or she is going to study for the next couple of years, whereas 'memorising and reproducing' might be perfectly sufficient for someone giving a welcome address in place of an indisposed colleague. Thus a well-informed attitude towards different concepts of learning is an important basis for thinking about metacognition.

9.3 Lifeworld: The social and material environment

Lifeworld is one of the most important terms in phenomenological philosophy. This branch of nineteenth/twentieth-century philosophy is generally not easy to understand, and neither is the concept of lifeworld. Nevertheless, it has been adopted in a variety of contexts in the social sciences, including education. This is due in part to its huge explanatory power, and in part to the fact that many of the philosophical considerations that make up its complexity may be disregarded without losing too much of the value of the concept with respect to social situations. The following sections, therefore, refer to a specific concept of lifeworld defined as follows.

> **Keyword: Everyday lifeworld**
>
> Everyday lifeworld isthe province of reality in which man continuously participates in ways which are at once inevitable and patterned. The everyday lifeworld is the region of reality in which man can engage himself and which he can change while he operates in it by means of his animate organism... . [It is] that province of reality which the wide-awake and normal adult simply takes for granted in the attitude of common sense. By this taken-for-grantedness, we designate everything which we experience as unquestionable; every state of affairs is for us unproblematic until further notice. (Schütz & Luckmann, 1973, p. 3–4)

This concept obviously addresses issues we dealt with in previous chapters. Temporality, for example, is part of the lifeworld (cf. ibid, pp. 45ff.), as is the experience of the lived body. (In the quotation above, *Leib* was translated as 'animate organism'.) Thus as a further limitation for the following considerations, lifeworld shall refer to the material and social surroundings *as experienced by the person*. This approach has proven useful in pedagogy and other areas that deal with the concept of learning, as stated by Roth:

Increasingly cognitive scientists agree that to understand knowing and learning, one needs to make person-in-situation the fundamental unit of analysis ... . Here, the 'situation' is not given in an absolute sense, for example, by a scientific description of the physical setting (including the 'task'), but by the situation as it appears to the person. (Roth, 2004, p. 10)

Yet the first link we can draw between the lifeworld and our discussions up to this point is not related to cognitive aspects, but to emotion. As Gieseke clearly pointed out, emotions play a crucial role in setting up and maintaining our relationship to others; they are part of the 'social arrangement of the lifeworld of everyday existence' (Schütz & Luckmann, 1973, p. 59). On the other hand, situational aspects influence people's emotions, which might very well cause them to avoid certain situations. And, as discussed earlier, emotions have an impact on both bodily and cognitive processes. Illeris's learning triangle translates this fact into a scheme: its lower corner (environment) has connections to both cognition and emotion, and these two are linked as well, because they are integrated in the whole person. So a first point to note is that learning will be fostered by circumstances that individuals experience in a way that allows them to engage emotionally without having to fear overly unpleasant consequences. Engaging with the environment should provide desirable prospects. In Gieseke's terms, being unable to engage emotionally with our environment would diminish the very dimensions of the lifeworld, whereas having to fear negative consequences would reduce our willingness to engage with it in the first place.

On this basis, the cognitive situation of the person-in-the-world can be further investigated. In this respect, we can clearly distinguish between two opposing perspectives. In the first perspective, knowledge about the world is regarded as something that exists in an objective way and can, to a greater or lesser extent, be acquired by the individual. Learning, according to this view, would mean *transmission* (Kolb & Kolb, 2005, p. 194; Reece & Walker 2003, p. 63). In the second perspective, the concept of the lifeworld, what counts for the individual is not a unique objective world, but the world as experienced. Experience, however, is determined by relationships. Knowledge about the world, therefore, can only mean knowledge about the world as experienced by the individual. Hence learning, according to this view, is regarded as *construction*. Although the term *constructivism* is rather young (and authors such as Kolb apply it to this perspective retrospectively, see Kolb & Kolb, 2005, p. 194), the perspective itself is much older. The following quotation by Kurt Lewin illustrates how the constructivist view dilutes the strict sense of objectivity adopted from natural sciences:

A teacher will never succeed in giving proper guidance to a child if he does not learn to understand the psychological world in which the individual child lives. To describe a situation 'objectively' in psychology actually means to describe the situation as a totality of those facts, and of only those facts, which make up the field of the individual. To substitute for that world of the individual the world of the teacher, of the physicist, or of anybody else is to be, not objective, but wrong. (Lewin, 1951, p. 62)

This statement evidently supports the position of phenomenography – which is not surprising, as phenomenographers use a phenomenological approach to examine cognitive processes. To facilitate learning thus means to contribute to an appropriate emotional situation and to support learners in finding, challenging, and developing their own 'truth' instead of presenting an allegedly objective one, however sophisticated it may be.

From the phenomenological point of view, this conclusion gives us an idea of how the individual may perceive and process impressions from the environment, and it suggests a number of corresponding 'didactic situations' (see Chapter 7.1). However, the relationship goes both ways. Cognitive processes, emotions, and bodily effects are induced by experienced circumstances, but the individual's reactions may likewise have an effect on the circumstances. Any kind of communication could serve as an example, because obviously, any contribution from a participant in a communication situation may have an effect on the others and thereby influence the process. On a large scale, learners' reactions and their effects on their lifeworld may have an influence on deeper levels of the environment, for example in the form of political participation. Evidently, this is a particular concern of pragmatism that has been discussed by Gieseke and others. This concern, again, has immediate consequences in terms of didactics. As soon as teaching and learning are no longer regarded as isolated phenomena within a closed province of formal learning, but as social processes situated in and mandated by society, the resulting effects evidently have to be taken into consideration. The phenomenological approach expands this perspective by stressing the point that it is the individual alone who actually experiences his or her situation in the world and ultimately decides what is desirable from this point of view. Yet, mutual action and learning can be facilitated, because individuals experience different viewpoints and learning aims by encountering others in the learning situation.

Exercises and tasks

Exercise 1

Recall the differences between *Leib*/lived body and body. What would teaching be like, in terms of its observable characteristics, if the teacher tried to take account of the body, the *Leib*, or neither of the two?

Exercise 2

Recall your previous learning experiences. Did you ever have the feeling that your teacher was talking about a world fundamentally different from what you experience as your lifeworld? Explain the differences you noticed.

Exercise 3

Imagine you were asked not to teach but to *confuse* other adult learners regarding a certain subject matter. How could you do so – not by saying wrong things, but simply by trying not to say things in a way that your students can relate to their lifeworld?

Task 1

Compare Kolb's 'learning style inventory' (see Tasks 1 and 2, Chapter 5) to the deep/surface approach to learning. You may find Coffield et al. (2004, see below) helpful for this task.

Coffield, F., Moseley, D., Hall, E., & Ecclestone, K. (2004). *Should we be using learning styles?* London: Learning and Skills Research Centre. Available at http://www.scribd.com/doc/20311529/Should-We-Be-Using-Learning-Styles

Task 2

After having explored the aspects of time, lived body, and lifeworld a bit further, you may now want to return to Task 1 in Chapter 3. What further terms or concepts do you consider to be useful for exploiting phenomenology with respect to a contemporary theory of learning?

http://www.phenomenologyonline.com

10. Conclusions

As announced in the introduction, the second part of this text is not intended to present a list of didactic rules to support or even secure good teaching practice. Like other professionals, a learning facilitator can make use of a variety of techniques, standardised methods, media, and the like, and will still need a certain artistic talent to practice the 'art of teaching', as Comenius famously put it in a much-quoted phrase. Thus the following paragraphs are intended as a guide to the conclusions we have drawn against the background of the theories and concepts discussed in previous chapters. If you have read this study guide all the way up to this final chapter, you certainly know too much about the facilitating character of teaching and the pedagogic foundations of the concept of learning to expect to be given a convenient checklist of simple, easy-to-use rules for teaching. The following summary is only meant to serve as a reminder, to review once more the important implications that a serious treatment of *learning theory* may have on *activities related to teaching*. I hope these conclusions will support you as you engage in the ongoing project of becoming and being an adult educator.

Conclusions regarding time: Obviously, teaching requires paying attention to the time that is necessary for completing a task. This may be done by reflecting on time expenditure with respect to the situation of the learners by

- counselling learners in their resource planning with respect to time
- individualising the learning situation in a way that allows different learners to allocate their time to different tasks according to their individual needs
- setting fixed points during the course to get the group of learners together and let them experience their progress *as a group*.

Conducting group discussions on time expenditure can help prevent discrepancies in learners' time budgets (in both directions, i.e. too much or too little time) and increase each learner's awareness of the necessity to keep track of the time available for completing different tasks. Furthermore, such discussions prevent teachers from making the often questionable assumption that they could precisely predict time requirements without asking their learners. Generally, teaching requires a sensitive attitude with respect to time. Having learners' time at one's command, as is usually the case in adult education, is a serious responsibility that should not be taken lightheartedly.

Conclusions regarding the person: Emotions are crucial in any teaching-learning process. Positive emotions regarding the learning matter or the situation may influence the process in positive ways. However, negative emotions, such as experiencing disjuncture, may sometimes be necessary to release further energy that will help keep learners engaged in the process. The only general guidance to be provided here, therefore, may be that positive emotions are usually supportive and that negative emotions should be avoided as long as they are not clearly required to propel the learning process. This may be achieved by

- being emotionally competent – that is, by being able to deal with learners' emotions constructively
- acting respectfully and allowing further emotions to appear and to be expressed during the learning process
- allowing emotions to contribute to the formation and maintenance of a learning group
- supporting learners in discovering approaches that come along with positive emotions
- supporting learners in encountering and integrating the emotional quality of learning processes.

Although there are strategies for dealing with certain emotional 'challenges', the emotional side of teaching is an area that particularly calls for teachers' *self-development*. There is nothing to say against using recommended strategies as long as they are used to accompany a process of ongoing self-development and growth (and not used to replace such a process). So the foremost way of dealing appropriately with emotions in teaching situations is to become aware of one's own emotions as a teacher and to continuously strive to improve one's own emotional competence.

The lived body is another important aspect of the person as learner. Although bodily requirements vary vastly with the actual learning task, a few fundamental implications exist due to the fact that the body, in part, *is* the person. Some approaches to address these implications include

110

- keeping in mind that, even as they sit motionless and silent, both learners and teachers are beings who are present with their lived body (sitting motionless is *a decision*, not a 'natural' state)
- providing opportunities for movement
- providing approaches towards the learning matter that allow learners to experience it in a bodily way
- allowing the bodily aspect of the person to support social learning.

The educational tradition generally has either neglected the body or regarded bodily aspects of learning as a special concern to be addressed by physical education classes, for instance. As a consequence, learners are often not aware of the bodily side of learning at all. This is one of the reasons for a variety of psychosomatic secondary effects of learning and teaching. Although they should be taken very seriously, they still tend to regard the body merely as a potential obstacle to learning that must be addressed to prevent it from disturbing the process. Yet there is hope that a more fundamental approach will emerge that will, first of all, simply acknowledge the presence of the body as an essential aspect of the person before categorising it as useful or problematic. However, since we still have a long way to go in this respect, addressing the body from a teacher's standpoint has to be done sensitively and carefully, as learners often are just not accustomed to this.

The cognitive side, even though it is a bit overrated in comparison to the other two, obviously still must be regarded as crucial for learning, especially for the learning of adolescents and adults. Some of the theory-related measures to support cognitive learning include

- distinguishing between a deep approach and a surface approach; both may be applicable, and it is not at all up to the teacher to decide which approach should be used (not normatively, but even less so in practice)
- introducing learners to both approaches and teaching them how to recognise which approach they are following, how to decide which approach is appropriate with respect to their aims, and how to pursue the corresponding strategies
- encouraging students to learn sustainably by offering them opportunities to challenge the learning matter in a maximum variety of ways
- creating an environment in which mistakes are not regarded as failures but as opportunities to further explore the matter, or even as suggestions to see it from a different angle by questioning assumptions previously taken for granted.

Conclusions regarding the lifeworld: The lifeworld is not just a certain perspective on things that teachers need to respect while teaching. It is the very world the learner inhabits – just as any teacher inhabits his or her lifeworld. The individual's learning takes place *within* this world, although it may eventually change it, of course. Teaching, therefore, doesn't mean changing the learner's lifeworld but creating a situation in which the learning incident is connected to, or part of, the learner's lifeworld. This may sound like a rather sophisticated socio-technical effort, but some of the suggestions made to support this perspective of learning and teaching have become quite common. They include

- avoiding circumstances that keep the learner from encountering the learning matter as a whole person (e.g. suppressing emotions or provoking negative feelings such as fear)
- respecting the individual's view as his or her inescapable 'personal world' which is not yours to configure
- offering learning opportunities in which learners may try out new ideas instead of being expected to merely adopt them
- considering the impact of the individual learning effort beyond the boundaries of that individual's lifeworld. Learning often comes with a mandate from society, which is why it is expected to serve the needs of societal development.

Whether you are more inclined towards a radical constructivist world view or towards more moderate perspectives, the fact that each of us relies on our very personal view of the world is inescapable. Fortunately, there seems to be a considerable degree of overlap between these 'worlds', allowing us to communicate, to agree or disagree, and even to provide impulses that may provoke changes in others (or in ourselves). Any teaching effort is bound by this fact –once famously transformed into an aphorism used at the beginning of a lecture: 'I am responsible for what I say but not for what you hear.' (Rumour has it that it was Humberto Maturana, one of the founders of radical constructivism, who coined this statement.) Nevertheless, as mentioned before with respect to learning time, any teaching activity involves great responsibility. Since writing a study guide may very well be considered a teaching activity, I hope that reading this book has provided you with some new ideas and insights to further develop your approach towards adult education. If that is the case, the text has already fulfilled its mission.

Exercises

Exercise 1

Have a look at the lists of conclusions. Take each list and decide which points are most important to you. You may use the result as an additional perspective when evaluating your next teaching activity.

Exercise 2

Prioritising the lists is *one* way of customising them to suit your individual needs. Another would be to change their content. Decide which items are suitable the way they are. Which require a reformulation? And which items do you think should be added to cover all the important aspects?

Exercise 3

If you are satisfied with your personal list of theory-based demands on teaching, put it aside for a while. Review the items after two to four weeks and find out (a) whether you could still give some theoretical reason for each item, and (b) whether you still regard them as properly worded and important for teaching. If possible, do this exercise along with other students and compare your results.

Annotated Bibliography

Arnold, R. (2005). *Approaches to adult education*. Montevideo: Cinterfor/ILO.

Based on his wide-ranging experience in national as well as international adult education, Rolf Arnold provides a broad picture of the general adult education discussion.

Bateson, G. (1972). *Steps to an ecology of mind*. Chicago: Chicago University Press.

Bateson's articles, collected in this volume, are definitely not limited to the issue of learning. However, it is safe to say that they influenced the work of a huge variety of social scientists (among others) and that they continue to serve as a key point of reference for theoretical considerations with respect to education and learning.

Bélanger, P. (2011). *Theories in adult learning and education*. Opladen & Farmington Hills: Budrich.

The volume on learning theories by Paul Bélanger and the present book complement each other. Bélanger's book elaborates on concepts that are only mentioned briefly in this study guide and particularly emphasises the important relationship between learning and participation.

Coffield, F., Moseley, D., Hall, E., & Ecclestone, K. (2004). *Should we be using learning styles?* London: Learning and Skills Research Centre. Retrieved from http://www.scribd.com/doc/20311529/Should-We-Be-Using-Learning-Styles

A short and yet insightful presentation of learning styles, their benefits, and their side effects.

Comenius, J. A. (1657/1967). *Great didactic* (M. W. Keatinge, Trans.). New York: Russel & Russel.

The *Didactica Magna* is one of the rather few real classics, and some of its ideas may still be linked to modern education research. Though Comenius's ideas about adult learners are not always encouraging, the book itself is doubtlessly worth reading – for example, to gain an impression of what has changed in education during modernisation and what has not. The edition quoted here also provides an insightful introduction by M. W. Keatinge.

Dewey, J. (1916). *Democracy and education: An introduction to the philosophy of education*. Retrieved from http://www.gutenberg.org/ebooks/852

Democracy and Education is another classic which should be recognised for its innovative and progressive ideas. It may also serve as a benchmark to refer to when dealing with contemporary concepts of (adult) learning.

Finger, M., & Asún, J. M. (2001). *Adult education at the crossroads*. Leicester: NIACE.

Finger and Asún managed to give an impressively comprehensive, and yet brief and inspiring, overview on the situation of adult education, ranging from fundamental theoretical considerations to political and economic aspects.

Gieseke, W. (2007). *Lebenslanges Lernen und Emotionen* [Lifelong learning and emotions]. Bielefeld: W. Bertelsmann.

Unfortunately, this volume is only available in German. To readers proficient in German, it provides a broad and deep approach to adult learning with an emphasis on emotions on the one hand and on relations on the other.

Göhlich, M., & Zirfas, J. (2007). *Lernen: Ein pädagogischer Grundbegriff* [Learning: A basic term in education]. Stuttgart: Kohlhammer.

This volume by Göhlich and Zirfas is another book that is only available in German. Among other issues, it provides a good argument for treating *learning* as a fundamental term in education. Furthermore, the authors trace some of the term's relations and boundaries to other (particularly psychological) concepts. Thus their approach is mostly concerned with the specificities of German terminology. However, Göhlich and Zirfas do an excellent job here, and of course also explore issues beyond this.

Hudson, B., & Schneuwly, B. (2007). Didactics: Learning and teaching in Europe. *European Educational Research Journal*, *6(2)*, 106–108.

The authors wrote one of the rare discussions of the term *didactic* in an international perspective. The text serves as an introduction to a special issue of the *Educational Research Journal*.

Illeris, K. (2004). *Adult education and adult learning*. Malabar, FL: Krieger.

Knud Illeris is one of the featured scholars in this text, and *Adult Education and Adult Learning* is one of the major books to comprehensively showcase his ideas.

Jarvis, P. (2006): *Towards a comprehensive theory of human learning*. London, New York: Routledge.

This book by Peter Jarvis collects and structures some of the main influences and conclusions the author has taken into account when dealing with learning theory.

116

Klafki, W. (1998). Characteristics of critical-constructive didaktik. In B. Gundem & S. Hopmann (Eds.), *Didaktik and/or curriculum: An international dialogue* (pp. 307–330). New York: Peter Lang.

Klafki's in-depth considerations of didactics, learning, *Bildung,* and the relationship of these three concepts may inspire any discussion in the field of adult as well as general education.

LeFrançois, G. (2005). *Theories of learning: What the old woman said.* Florence, KY: Wadsworth.

The 'old woman', invented by LeFrançois for didactical reasons, gives a comprehensive introduction to *psychological* learning theory. Even though she sometimes does so in a rather unconventional way, her arguments are always precise and appropriate.

Marton, F., Hounsell, D., & Entwistle, N. (Eds.). (2005). *The experience of learning: Implications for teaching and studying in higher education* (3rd (Internet) ed.). Edinburgh. Retrieved from http://www.tla.ed.ac.uk/resources/EoL.html

This online edition of an older book by Marton, Hounsell, and Entwhistle provides a variety of important basic texts on variation theory, or phenomenography.

Meyer-Drawe, K. (2008). *Diskurse des Lernens* [Discourses of learning]. Munich: W. Fink.

The last of the German language books in this list deals with discourses of learning from a dedicated philosophical point of view. Käte Meyer-Drawe unfolds her immense knowledge on learning with particular respect to phenomenology. She also discusses contemporary (and critical) views on neuroscience approaches.

Ryan, R. M., & Deci, E. L. (2000). Self-determination theory and the facilitation of intrinsic motivation, social development, and well-being. *American Psychologist, 55(1),* 68–78.

The self-determination theory of motivation still is a primary reference when dealing with the relationship between learning and motivation. Its particular strength lies in the fact that it addresses the motivational factors that are relevant and influential in pedagogical situations.

Von Glasersfeld, E. (1995). *Radical constructivism: A way of knowing and learning.* London: Falmer.

Though constructivism is essentially an epistemological theory, it is also being discussed as a kind of learning theory. The fundamental assumptions of constructivism are presented in this book by one of its 'founding fathers'. What is notable about Glasersfeld's work is that he usually seeks to connect his thoughts to the inspirational work of Jean Piaget rather than putting constructivism in harsh opposition to Piaget's cognitive approach.

References

Abbott, E. A. (n.d./1884). *Flatland: A romance of many dimensions.* Retrieved from http://www.geom.uiuc.edu/~banchoff/Flatland/

Ausubel, D. P. (1960). The use of advance organizers in the learning and retention of meaningful verbal material. *Journal of Educational Psychology, 51,* 267–272.

Arnold, R. (2005). *Approaches to adult education.* Montevideo: Cinterfor/ILO.

Arnold, R., & Pätzold, H. (2007). *Schulpädagogik kompakt* [Essentials of school pedagogy]. Berlin: Cornelsen-Scriptor.

Arnold, R., & Pätzold, H. (2008). *Bausteine zur Erwachsenenbildung* [Contributions to adult education]. Baltmannsweiler: Schneider.

Basfeld, M. (2008). Wieviel Sinne hat der Mensch [How many senses does man have]. In R. Grimm, & G. Kaschubowski (Eds.), *Kompendium der anthroposophischen Heilpädagogik* (pp. 200–212). Munich: Ernst Reinhardt.

Bateson, G. (1972). *Steps to an ecology of mind.* Chicago: Chicago University Press.

Bélanger, P. (2011). *Theories in adult learning and education.* Opladen & Farmington Hills: Budrich.

Berger, P. L., & Luckmann, T. (1966). *The social construction of reality: A treatise in the sociology of knowledge.* Garden City, NY: Anchor Books.

Biesta, G. (2009, March). Educational research, democracy and TLRP. Lecture presented at the TLRP event Methodological Development, Future Challenges, London, United Kingdom. Retrieved from http://www.tlrp.org/dspace/handle/123456789/1620

Biggs, J., & Collis, K. (1982). *Evaluating the quality of learning: The SOLO taxonomy.* New York: Academy Press.

Brousseau, G. (1998). *Théorie des situations didactique* [Theory of didactic situations]. Grenoble: La Pensée Sauvage.

Bruer, J. T. (2008). In search of … brain-based education. In Jossey-Brass Publishers (Ed.), *The Jossey Bass reader on the brain and learning* (pp. 51–69). San Francisco: Jossey-Brass.

Bullock, D. H. (1987). *Programmed instruction.* Englewood Cliffs, NJ: Educational Technology Publications.

Chevallard, Y. (2007). Readjusting didactics to a changing epistemology. *European Educational Research Journal, 6(2),* 131–134.

Coffield, F., Moseley, D., Hall, E., & Ecclestone, K. (2004). *Should we be using learning styles?* London: Learning and Skills Research Centre. Retrieved from http://www.scribd.com/doc/20311529/Should-We-Be-Using-Learning-Styles

Collins, A., Brown, J. S., & Newman, S. F. (1989). Cognitive apprenticeship: Teaching the crafts of reading, writing and mathematics. In L. B. Resnick (Ed.), *Knowing, learning, and instruction: Essays in honor of Robert Glaser* (pp. 453–494). Hillsdale: Lawrence Erlbaum.

Colombetti, G., & Thompson, E. (2007). The feeling body: Towards an enactive approach to emotion. In W.F. Overton, U. Müller, & J. Newman (Eds.), *Body in mind, mind in body: Developmental perspectives on embodiment and consciousness* (pp. 45–68). Philadelphia: Lawrence Erlbaum.

Comenius, J. A. (1657/1967). *Great didactic* (M. W. Keatinge, Trans.). New York: Russel & Russel.

Dahlgren, L.-O. (2005). Learning conceptions and outcomes. In F. Marton, D. Hounsell, & N. Entwistle (Eds.), *The experience of learning: Implications for teaching and studying in higher education* (pp. 23–38). Edinburgh: Scottish Academic Press.

Dewey, J. (1916). *Democracy and education: An introduction to the philosophy of education.* Retrieved from http://www.gutenberg.org/ebooks/852

Dewey, J. (1911). Didactics. In P. Monroe (Ed.), *A cyclopedia of education* (Vol. 2, p. 327). New York: MacMillan.

Deutsches Institut für Erwachsenenbildung (DIE) (2011). *Lernen in Bewegung* [Learning in motion, complete issue]. *DIE-Zeitschrift für Erwachsenenbildung, 1.*

Faulstich, P., & Grell, P. (2004). Lernwiderstände beim 'selbstbestimmten Lernen' [Learning resistance in self-directed learning]. In W. Bender, M. Groß, & H. Heglmeier (Eds.), *Lernen und Handeln: Eine Grundfrage der Erwachsenenbildung* (pp. 107–123). Schwalbach/Taunus: Wochenschau.

Finger, M., & Asún, J. M. (2001). *Adult education at the crossroads.* Leicester: NIACE.

Flowers, R. (Ed.). (2009). Popular education [Complete issue]. *Report: Zeitschrift für Weiterbildungsforschung, 32(2).*

Freiler, Tammy J. (2008). Learning through the body. In S. B. Merriam (Ed.), *Third update on adult learning theory* (pp. 37–47). San Francisco, CA: Jossey-Bass.

Friesen, N. (2007). (Micro-)didactics: A tale of two traditions. In T. Hug (Ed.), *Didactics of microlearning* (pp. 83–97). Münster: Waxmann.

Gallese, V. (2005). Embodied simulation: From neurons to phenomenal experience. *Phenomenology and the Cognitive Science, 4,* 23–48.

Gallese, V., Eagle, M. N., & Migone, P. (2007). Intentional attunement: Mirror neurons and the neural underpinnings of interpersonal relations. *Journal of the American Psychoanalytical Association, 55(1),* 132–176.

Gallese, V., Keysers, C., & Rizzolatti, G. (2004). A unifying view of the basis of social cognition. *TRENDS in Cognitive Sciences, 8(9),* 396–403.

Geulen, D., & Hurrelmann, K. (1980). Zur Programmatik einer umfassenden Sozialisationstheorie [Towards a comprehensive theory of socialisation]. In K. Hurrelmann, & D. Ulich (Eds.), *Handbuch der Sozialisationsforschung* (pp. 51–67). Weinheim: Beltz.

Gieseke, W. (2007). *Lebenslanges Lernen und Emotionen* [Lifelong learning and emotions]. Bielefeld: W. Bertelsmann.

Giesinger, J. (2006). Erziehung der Gehirne: Willensfreiheit, Hirnforschung und Pädagogik [Educating brains: Freedom of the will, neuroscience, and pedagogy]. *Zeitschrift für Erziehungswissenschaft, 9(1)*, 97–109.

Göhlich, M., & Zirfas, J. (2007). *Lernen: Ein pädagogischer Grundbegriff* [Learning: A basic term in education]. Stuttgart: Kohlhammer.

Günther, G. (1991). *Idee und Grundriss einer nicht-aristotelischen Logik* [Idea and outline of non-Aristotelian logic]. Berlin: Akademie.

Halloway, W. (n.d.). *Quality learning with reference to the SOLO model.* Retrieved from http://www.une.edu.au/education/research/bhutan/publications/bhutan-solo-halloway.pdf.

Herbart, J. F. (1806/1992). Einleitung in die Allgemeine Pädagogik [Introduction to general pedagogy]. In H. Scheurl (Ed.), *Lust an der Erkenntnis: Die Pädagogik der Moderne* (pp. 155–162). Munich: Pieper.

Hodkinson, P., Biesta, G., & James, D. (2008). Understanding learning culturally: Overcoming the dualism between social and individual views of learning. *Vocations and Learning, 1*, 27–47.

Holzkamp, K. (1995). *Lernen. Subjektwissenschaftliche Grundlegung* [Learning: Subject-scientific foundations]. Frankfurt/Main: Campus.

Hudson, B. (2007). Comparing different traditions of teaching and learning: What can we learn about teaching and learning? *European Educational Research Journal, 6(2)*, 136–146.

Hudson, B., & Schneuwly, B. (2007). Didactics: Learning and teaching in Europe. *European Educational Research Journal, 6(2)*, 106–108.

Illeris, K. (2003). Towards a contemporary and comprehensive theory of learning. *International Journal of Lifelong Education, 22(4)*, 396–406.

Illeris, K. (2004). *Adult education and adult learning.* Malabar, FL: Krieger.

Illeris, K. (2006). Das 'Lerndreieck': Rahmenkonzept für ein übergreifendes Verständnis vom menschlichen Lernen [The learning triangle. Framework for a comprehensive understanding of human learning]. In E. Nuissl (Ed.), *Vom Lernen zum Lehren: Lern- und Lehrforschung für die Weiterbildung* (pp. 29–41). Bielefeld: W. Bertelsmann.

Jank, W., & Meyer, H. (2009). *Didaktische Modelle* [Didactic models] (9th ed.). Berlin: Cornelsen.

Jarvis, P. (2006): *Towards a comprehensive theory of human learning.* London, New York: Routledge.

Jarvis, P. (2008): *Learning to be a person in society.* London, New York: Routledge.

Keatinge, M. W. (1967). Biographical introduction. In J.A. Comenius, *Great didactic* (M.W. Keatinge, Trans.) (pp.1–101). New York: Russel & Russel.

Klafki, W. (1998). Characteristics of critical-constructive didaktik. In B. Gundem, & S. Hopmann (Eds.), *Didaktik and/or curriculum: An international dialogue* (pp. 307–330). New York: Peter Lang.

Klafki, W. (1985). *Neue Studien zur Bildungstheorie und Didaktik* [New studies on education theory and didactics]. Weinheim:

Knowles, M. S. (1975). *Self-directed learning: A guide for learners and teachers.* Englewood Cliffs: Prentice Hall.

Knowles, M. S., Holton III, E. F., & Swanson, R. A. (2005). *The adult learner* (6th ed.). London: Elsevier.

Koch, L. (1988). Überlegungen zum Begriff und zur Logik des Lernens [Thoughts on the idea and the logic of learning]. *Zeitschrift für Pädagogik, 34(3)*, 315–330.

Kolb, D. (1984). *Experiential learning.* Englewood Cliffs: Prentice Hall.

Kolb, D. A., & Kolb, A. Y. (2005). Learning styles and learning spaces: Enhancing experiential learning in higher education. *Academy of Management Learning & Education, 4(2)*, 193–212.

Lave, J. (1977). Tailor-made experiments and evaluating the intellectual consequences of apprenticeship training. *The Quarterly Newsletter of the Institute for Comparative Human Development, 1*, 1–3.

Lave, J., & Wenger, E. (1991). *Situated learning: Legitimate peripheral participation.* New York: Cambridge University Press.

LeFrançois, G. (2005). *Theories of learning: What the old woman said.* Florence, KY: Wadsworth.

Lewin, K. (1951). *Field theory in social science.* New York: Harper & Row.

Libet, B. (1978). Neuronal vs. subjective timing for a conscious sensory experience. In P. A. Buser, & A. Rougeul-Buser (Eds.), *Cerebral correlations of conscious experience* (pp. 69–82). Amsterdam: Elsevier.

Luhmann, N. (1995), *Social systems.* Stanford: Stanford University Press.

Luhmann, N. (2004). *Schriften zur Pädagogik* [Writings on Pedagogy]. D. Lenzen (Ed.). Frankfurt am Main: Suhrkamp.

Lund, A. (2003). *The teacher as interface* (Doctoral dissertation, University of Oslo, Norway). Retrieved from the University of Oslo website: http://www.uv.uio.no/ils/forskning/publikasjoner/rapporter-og-avhandlingen/AndreasLund-avhandling%5B1%5D.pdf

Marton, F. (1992). Phenomenography and 'the art of teaching all things to all men'. *Qualitative Studies in Education, 5(3)*, 253–265.

Marton, F., Dall'Alba, G., & Beaty E. (1993). Conceptions of learning. *International Journal of Educational Research, 19*, 277–300.

Marton, F., Hounsell, D., & Entwistle, N. (Eds.). (2005). *The experience of learning: Implications for teaching and studying in higher education* (3rd (internet) ed.). Edinburgh. Retrieved from http://www.tla.ed.ac.uk/resources/EoL.html

Marton, F., & Pang, M. F. (1999, August). Two faces of variation. Paper presented at the 8th European Conference for Learning and Instruction, Gothenburg, Sweden. Retrieved from http://www.ped.gu.se/biorn/phgraph/civil/graphica/fmpmf.pdf

Marton, F., & Säljö, R. (2005). Approaches to learning. In F. Marton, D. Hounsell, & N. Entwistle (Eds.), *The experience of learning: Implications for teaching and studying in higher education* (pp. 39–58). Edinburgh: Scottish Academic Press.

Merton, R. (1957): The role-set: Problems in sociological theory. *British Journal of Sociology, 8(2)*, 106–120. Retrieved from http://www.jstor.org/stable/587363?seq=2.

Melander, H. (2009). *Trajectories of learning.* Uppsala: University of Uppsala.

Meyer-Drawe, K. (1996). Von anderen lernen. Phänomenologische Betrachtungen in der Pädagogik [Learning from others: Phenomenological reflections in pedagogy]. In M. Berelli, & J. Ruhloff (Eds.), *Deutsche Gegenwartspädagogik II* (pp. 85–98). Baltmannsweiler: Schneider.

Meyer-Drawe, K. (2003). Lernen als Erfahrung [Learning as experience]. *Zeitschrift für Erziehungswissenschaft, 6(4)*, 505–514.

Meyer-Drawe, K. (2008). *Diskurse des Lernens* [Discourses of learning]. Munich: W. Fink.

Niemi, H (2009). Why from teaching to learning? *European Educational Research Journal, 8(1)*, 1–17.

Pätzold, H. (2004). *Lernberatung und Erwachsenenbildung* [Learning advice and adult education]. Baltmannsweiler: Schneider.

Pätzold, H. (2008, September). Learning in the world: Towards a culturally aware concept of learning. Paper presented at the European Conference on Educational Research, Gothenburg, Sweden. Retrieved from http://www.eera-ecer.eu/fileadmin/user_upload/Publication_FULL_TEXTS/ECER2008_244_P%C3%A4tzold.pdf.

Pätzold, H. (2010a). Strukturelle Kopplung, Konstruktivismus und Spiegelneuronen: Neue Erklärungsmöglichkeiten für das Phänomen Lernen [Structural linkage, constructivism, and mirror neurons: New possibilities for explaining the phenomenon of learning]. *Pädagogische Rundschau, 64*, 405–417.

Pätzold, H. (2010b). Lernen lernen [Learning how to learn]. In R. Arnold, S. Nolda, & E. Nuissl (Eds.), *Wörterbuch Erwachsenenbildung* (2nd ed., pp. 194–196). Bad Heilbrunn: Klinkhardt.

Pätzold, H. (2010c). Responsibility and accountability in adult education: The unequal siblings. In R. Egetenmeyer, & E. Nuissl (Eds.), *Teachers and trainers in adult and lifelong learning: Asian and European perspectives* (pp. 135–143). Frankfurt: Peter Lang.

Pätzold, H. (2011). Emotions, the person and the 'lived body': Learning experiences and impacts from the 'pedagogical orientation'. *ROSE: Research on Steiner Education, 2(1)*, 48–55. Available at http://www.rosejourn.com/index.php/rose/article/viewFile/62/90.

Pearson, E. M., & Podeschi, R. L. (1999). Humanism and individualism: Maslow and his critics. *Adult Education Quarterly, 50(1)*, 41–55.

Rabil, A. (n.d.). Humanism 1: An outline. Retrieved from http://www.globaled.org/nyworld/materials/humanism/H1.html.

Reece, I., & Walker, S. (2003). *Teaching, training and learning* (5th ed.). Sunderland: Business Educator's Publishers.

Rehrl, M., & Gruber, H. (2007). Netzwerkanalyse in der Pädagogik [Network analysis in pedagogy]. *Zeitschrift für Pädagogik, 53(2)*, 243–264.

Rizzolatti, G., & Sinigaglia, C. (2008). *Mirrors in the brain: How our minds share actions and emotions.* Oxford: Oxford University Press.

Roth, W.-M. (2004). Cognitive phenomenology: Marriage of phenomenology and cognitive science. *Forum: Qualitative Social Research, 5.* Retrieved from http://www.qualitative-research.net/index.php/fqs

Ryan, R. M., & Deci, E. L. (2000). Self-determination theory and the facilitation of intrinsic motivation, social development, and well-being. *American Psychologist, 55(1)*, 68–78.

Ryle, G. (1949/1990): *The concept of mind.* London: Penguin.

Schäffter, O. (2010). Institutionalformen für lebenslanges Lernen: Eckpunkte eines erwachsenenpädagogischen Forschungsprogramms [Types of institutions for lifelong learning: Key issues for a research programme in adult education]. In K. Dollhausen, T. Feld, & W. Seitter (Eds.), *Erwachsenenpädagogische Organisationsforschung* (pp. 293–316). Wiesbaden: Verlag für Sozialwissenschaften.

Schütz, A., & Luckmann, T. (1973). *The structures of the life-world.* Evanston, Ill.: Northwest University Press.

Siebert, H. (2010). *Methoden für die Bildungsarbeit* [Methods for working in education]. Bielefeld: W. Bertelsmann.

Skirbekk, G., & Gilje, N. (2001). *A history of western thought.* New York: Routledge.

Smith, P. J., & Blake, D. (2009). The influence of learning environment on student conceptions of learning. *Journal of Vocational Education and Training, 61(3)*, 231–246.

St. Clair, R. (2004). A beautiful friendship? The relationship of research to practice in adult education. *Adult Education Quarterly, 3*, 224–241.

Thompson, E., & Zahavi, D. (2007). Philosophical issues: Phenomenology. In D. P. Zelazo, M. Moscovitch, & E. Thompson (Eds.), *The Cambridge handbook of consciousness* (pp. 67–87). New York: Cambridge University Press.

Unwin, L. (2008). Shaping teaching and learning in TVET. In F. Rauner, & R. McLean (Eds.), *Handbook of technical and vocational education and training research* (pp. 508–511). Berlin: Springer.

Visser, M. (2003). Gregory Bateson on deutero-learning and double bind: A brief conceptual history. *Journal of History of the Behavioral Sciences, 39(3)*, 269–278.

van der Loo, H., & van Rejen, W. (1992). *Modernisierung: Projekt und Paradox* [Modernisation: Project and paradox]. Munich: dtv.

von Foerster, H. (1972). Responsibility of competence. *Journal of Cybernetics, 2*, 1–6.

von Glasersfeld, E. (1995). *Radical constructivism: A way of knowing and learning.* London: Falmer.

About the Author

Dr. Henning Pätzold, M.A., has been Professor of Education with an emphasis on research and development in organisations at the University of Koblenz-Landau, Campus Koblenz, Germany, since 2011. Before coming to Koblenz, he was a professor of general education at the Freie Hochschule Mannheim and an assistant professor at the University of Kaiserslautern.

Henning Pätzold studied education, social sciences, and mathematics at the University of Kaiserslautern. After being licensed as a secondary school teacher, he gave courses in adult education for some time and then returned to the university to pursue his doctoral degree in education. He was engaged in several research projects, ranging from e-learning to European adult education, where he was engaged in the EMAE-project (European Master of Adult Education), coordinated by the University of Duisburg-Essen. His further research interests are learning theory, organisational learning, professionalism, and educational responsibility.

Since 2008, Henning Pätzold has been a senior researcher at the German Institute of Adult Education (DIE) in Bonn, where he is co-directing the programme on professionalism and professionalisation in adult education. His professional memberships include the German Society for Educational Science (DGfE) and the European Society for Research on the Education of Adults (ESREA).

Index

Our new series
Study Guides in Adult Education

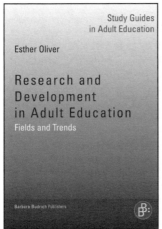

ESTHER OLIVER

Research and Development in Adult Education

Fields and Trends

Study Guides in Adult Education

2010. 135 pp. Pb. 16,90 € (D), 17,40 € (A), 25,90 SFr, US$ 25.95, GBP 15,95

ISBN 978-3-86649-304-9

The importance of adult education has been growing steadily, whether it's with regard to migration, societal inclusion, the work place, or the professionalization of adult educators themselves. By providing an international perspective on the most important research issues in adult education, this study guide offers a wealth of up-to-date information for anyone interested in this diverse field. The book is designed as a text book providing didactic material for discussion and further exploration of a wide range of adult education research from an international perspective.

Verlag Barbara Budrich • Barbara Budrich Publishers
Stauffenbergstr. 7. D-51379 Leverkusen Opladen
Tel +49 (0)2171.344.594 • Fax +49 (0)2171.344.693 • info@budrich-verlag.de
US-office: Uschi Golden • 28347 Ridgebrook • Farmington Hills, MI 48334 • USA •
ph +1.248.488.9153 • info@barbara-budrich.net • www.barbara-budrich.net

www.barbara-budrich.net

Study Guides in Adult Education

PAUL BÉLANGER
Theories in Adult Learning and Education
2011. 106 pp. Pb. 12,90 €, US$ 19.95, GBP 12.95
ISBN 978-3-86649-362-9
The graduate student guide in adult education explores theories of adult learning and adult education participation. It provides a frame of reference for understanding the development of a rapidly evolving field and for enhancing knowledge and competencies in this professional domain. The publication is divided into two sections: a section on adult learning theories and a section on adult education participation theories.

LICÍNIO C. LIMA/PAULA GUIMARÃES
European Strategies in Lifelong Learning
A Critical Introduction
2011. 165 pp. Pb. 18,90 €
ISBN 978-3-86649-444-2
Lifelong learning is currently widely accepted in terms of its benefits, thus the meanings it can contain are rarely questioned. This book proposes three models for analysing public adult education policies, the *democratic-emancipatory model*, the *modernisation and state control model*, and the *human resources management model*. The book further describes the proposals presented by UNESCO since the 1970s with respect to lifelong education and lifelong learning. The underlying purpose of this approach is to identify

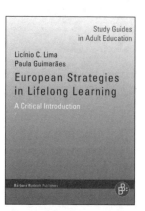

and interpret other meanings the idea may contain today. This option is intended to help students and other readers who may be interested in questioning current views on a priority issue in contemporary public policies.

Verlag Barbara Budrich • Barbara Budrich Publishers
Stauffenbergstr. 7. D-51379 Leverkusen Opladen
Tel +49 (0)2171.344.594 • Fax +49 (0)2171.344.693 • info@budrich-verlag.de
US-office: Uschi Golden • 28347 Ridgebrook • Farmington Hills, MI 48334 • USA •
ph +1.248.488.9153 • info@barbara-budrich.net • www.barbara-budrich.net

www.barbara-budrich.net